On the Road to
EMMAUS

STORIES OF

Faith, Doubt, and Change

MARK COLLINS

LIGUORI
PUBLICATIONS
One Liguori Drive
Liguori, MO 63057-9999
(314) 464-2500

Cover and interior art by Juliette Borda
Cover and interior design by Pam Hummelsheim

Contents

Acknowledgments

The author gratefully acknowledges the publishers of the following newspapers and magazines, where versions of these essays first appeared: *National Catholic Reporter, Pittsburgh Press, Pittsburgh Post-Gazette, The Journal of Teaching and Learning, The Jewish Chronicle, Pittsburgh Catholic,* and *Pitt Magazine.*

The author wishes to thank the departments of English, Library Science, and University Relations at the University of Pittsburgh for their continued support; Wanda Patrick at D.C. General for her guidance; and the reference staff at Carnegie Library of Pittsburgh for their incredible patience.

The author also acknowledges the help of several manuscript readers: Michael Kane, Mary Claire Dixon, Sally Ann Flecker, Cindy Collins, and Audrey Vest of Liguori Publications. While all five of these folks have agreed to take full responsibility for any errors of fact or opinion (and further agreed that they were personally responsible for the Watergate conspiracy), the author accepts all consequences for what is written in this book.

If I had the space, I would have thanked the following people whose questions—both solicited and otherwise—influenced the shaping of this book: Ralph Karsh, Michael McCabe, Wendy Wareham, Brian Pendergast, Dean Mougianis, Carrie Plazek, Jack Perry, Kevin Rippin, Debbie Koma, Sally Flecker, Todd Erkel, Alta Rusman, Laura Shefler, Emily Zeiders, Jeanne Marie Laskas, Elizabeth Drescher, Jim Ross, Linda Harper, Mary Kane, Edith Hughes, Marie Hughes, Jen, Art, Ron, Linda and Sharon; Michael Farrell, Michael McGough, Phil Taylor, Ed Wintermantel, Ann Metzger, Kit Ayars, Beth Newborg, Jeff Oaks, Virginia Phillips, Susan Stroyd, Eve Shelnutt, Chuck Kinder, Buddy Nordan, Art Craft, the Ladicks (all forty-three of them), the Woodses (all 212 of 'em), the Kanes (all 584 of ditto), J.P. Malochey, Robert Van Der Maalen, Ed Ochester, Lee Gutkind, Greg Pitlyk, Linda Smith Davis, Tom Chakurda, Renae Hardoby, Brian O'Neill, Arjuna Parakarma, Kristi Karsh, Elizabeth Mayer, Dave Smith, Mike Allen, Margaret Mary Kimmel, Gary and Megan Topolosky, Geeta Khotari, Paula Babac, Sharon Flake, Walter Watson, Tony Soltis, Bob Palmeri, Mary James, Sarah Williams, Jennifer Hall McKlay, Carol Sajko, Mark Shelton, John Fetterman.

Mark Collins

To my family: Mom and Dad,
Aunt Helen, Kevin and Cindy;
to my in-laws;
to my kids, Faith and Hope;

and to my wife, Sandee:
On the Avenue—Fifth Avenue—
the photographers will snap us, (click, click)
and you'll find that you're in the rotogravure.
Oh, I could write a sonnet...

All those things for which we have no words are lost.
The mind—the culture—has two little tools,
grammar and lexicon:
a decorated sand bucket and a matching shovel.
With these we bluster about the continents to
do all the world's work.
With these we try to save our very lives.

Annie Dillard
"Total Eclipse"

ON THAT SAME DAY two of Jesus' followers were going to a village named Emmaus, about seven miles from Jerusalem, and they were talking to each other about all the things that had happened. As they talked and discussed, Jesus himself drew near and walked with them; they saw him, but somehow did not recognize him.

LUKE 24:13-16

Foreword

In his spiritual classic, *Seeds of Contemplation,* Thomas Merton clearly pointed out where we might find holiness:

> *Every moment and every event of every man's life on earth plants something in his soul. For just as the wind carries thousands of winged seeds, so each moment brings with it germs of spiritual vitality that come to rest imperceptibly in the minds and wills of men. Most of these unnumbered seeds perish and are lost, because men are not prepared to receive them: for such seeds as these cannot spring up anywhere except in the good soil of freedom, spontaneity and love.*

In other words, Merton was pointing out that holiness is everywhere. Yet it is too often painfully apparent that we are not fertile ground for these seeds; in fact, we swat at them as they flutter down upon us or angrily trod them into the ground beneath our feet—feet that may be padding across a living-room carpet late at night or pounding along a concrete sidewalk on the way to work in the morning. It is difficult to see that daily occurrences, daily contacts, moments in which we seem to be furthest away from God, are indeed our seeds of contemplation, our seeds of insight, our seeds of redemption.

In Mark Collins' world—as in Merton's—these seeds, some fat with promise and others desiccated and unpromising, are squarely faced and boldly considered. Both writers are sure that there is a God who spends some time in the proper places—a church or a meditation room, for example—but *just as sure* that the God they struggled to know is with them in their daily experiences, ready to assist them in sorting out the jagged pieces that compose our lives.

From a husband's love for his wife with Alzheimer's to a jazz concert to a bleary evening in a topless bar, Mark Collins looks at the ordinary and makes it extraordinary. Picking up a Gideon Bible in a Ramada Inn in Altoona, Pennsylvania; talking to a friend dying of leukemia; learning that he will be a father—these are some of the seeds that have floated down upon Mark Collins. And because of his unremitting desire for contemplation and unrelenting sense of humor, he presents them here for our contemplation as well.

Mark Collins says, as he reflects on his own fits and starts, "Jesus was a lot of things, but consistent wasn't one of them." In these essays, we follow a man who also is not consistent—either in his beliefs or in his struggle to lead a good and decent life. But what he does cling to is the continuing need for the examined life, even though such examination can at times be humbling and painful.

"Life is a mysterious puzzle," Mark Collins writes. "The universe is like a child's car seat with the fake steering wheel. We try to navigate the turns and we beep our little plastic horn, but it's all a myth. Someone else is driving, and the best you can do is strap yourself in and enjoy the ride."

So, strap yourself in and enjoy this ride with Mark Collins at the wheel.

Paul Wilkes
Gilbertville, Massachusetts

Introduction:
Spare the Change,
Spoil the Child

In my senior year of college, I bought a 1974 VW Beetle. My father agreed to help me restore it. It needed a new everything, so our progress came in small victories, from loosening a rusted lug nut to plugging a leaky vacuum pump with a bread wrapper and bathroom caulking. On one calamitous night, my father tried to jump-start the engine by yanking the pulley belt.

"Just turn the key once," he called to me—and once was all it took. The engine started—well, nearly. But the belt pinched off the top half of my father's ring finger—well, completely.

The changes in *my* life have been less abrupt, but just as permanent.

Years later, in a therapist's office, I made the kind of revelation that nearly justified the outrageous hourly rate:

Change is brutal.

Change is our curse, the original payback for original sin. Unimpressed by Paradise, Eve sought change—ripe pickings for a snake with a ripe apple. So here we are, endlessly surprised by our changes, both sought and unsought. "If I only had more money (or a lover or a better boss or a higher IQ), then everything would be set," we say. "Then I could..." Could what? Be happy? Be a financially-and-emotionally-secure-yet-environmentally-conscious-well-rounded-well-liked-self-actualized-caring-and-competent-in-all-relationships-twenty-first-century-type-of-person?

You'd be better off with an apple.

Besides, preparation doesn't help. Change is too sudden. I'm sitting in the living room, minding my own business, watching the Pirates on cable when the phone rings. Uncle Harry died. Or my wallet's been stolen. Or it's been found, and all $4.72 is still there. Or I lost my job. Or found a job. Sometimes I think the military has the right idea: send a telegram. Unlike phone calls or television, telegrams give your brain a chance to offer options. "A telegram?" you say. "For me? Well, maybe Uncle Harry died...or *maybe I won $10 million from Publisher's Clearinghouse!*" Such delusion is an important part of denial, and denial is the basis of all hope. It's true.

Worse, change won't go away. Oh, sure, we still grimace at our social gaffes, some of which date back to the Nixon Administration. We all know misunderstandings happen, and—desperate to preserve our handful of friendships—we offer mutual apologies. Apology accepted, the air is cleared. Yet the suspicion remains: is the damage permanent?

Late at night, we wonder what happened to those magic moments of clarity and connection. Back then, it seemed like a lifetime friendship—or was it just the wine? Now you can't locate his number, and the Christmas cards stopped years ago. Does he ever think of you or that transcendent moment together? Or is the intimacy lost forever? That piece of your soul you shared that night—did it escape his memory? Is it circling the heavens like old radio waves from *Amos 'n' Andy*?

What follows in these pages is a chronicle of transcendent changes: birth, childhood, education, marriage, evil, loss, death, rebirth—the usual list of suspects. I'd love to tell you how much I've learned, but the truth is I'm more clueless than ever. Change—like love, like the universe—grows more complex with age. New wrinkles appear on old theories until you can't tell the compromises from the principles. Now I'm left with the jigsaw pieces of my past strewn about the hallways of my mind and unable to remember where I stored the box top with the pretty picture of how it all fits together.

Which reminds me: when my family went on vacation, I always got the seat in the cargo area of the station wagon—the "wayback" we called it, as in "way in the back." As the youngest, I wasn't consulted about seating, but the wayback was okay by me. I liked to see where we had come from rather than where we were headed. Besides, I was a great early-warning siren when one of the beach chairs became unmoored from the cartop carrier and went skidding into oncoming traffic on I-80.

I still like to watch where I've been, but I've lost more than beach chairs along the way. Whole sections of my past have ripped loose, despite my careful square knots. By sharing myself with you, dear reader, I'm hoping to keep some of it alive before it all breaks loose forever.

Shalom.

AS THE MOON ROSE HIGHER the inessential houses began to melt away until gradually I became aware of the old island here that flowered once for Dutch sailors' eyes—a fresh, green breast of the new world. Its vanished trees, the trees that had made way for Gatsby's house, had once pandered in whispers to the last and greatest of all human dreams; for a transitory enchanted moment man must have held his breath in the presence of this continent, compelled into an aesthetic contemplation he neither understood nor desired, face to face for the last time in history with something commensurate to his capacity for wonder.

        – THE GREAT GATSBY

Fear, Wonder, and Cranberry Sauce

FScott Fitzgerald was twenty-nine when he wrote the above lines in *The Great Gatsby*. He was already world-weary, having lived through war, poverty, rejection, and the kindling of his own wife's mental disintegration. Neither talent nor alcohol could change the burden of his conviction; by 1925 Fitzgerald thought America had seen it all.

He was half right. Through the rest of the "American century," technology would delight us and deliver us. But now, as we stand neck-deep in progress, it's more like drowning than deliverance. Each passing decade weakens our sense of wonder. Once you've seen one space rocket launched, haven't you seen them all? Is that Beirut they're showing on television, or is that Jerusalem? Or New York? Despite the sensational graphics and news reports, most Americans still can't remember which country is our friend or which religious leader has fallen or even what tastes great but is less filling. It's not because we've been told too little, but told too often. The Information Age has flooded our reservoir of knowledge with both pap and profundity, but the spillway can't manage the overflow.

So our saturated minds sit in front of the television, awash in facts and images but retaining nothing. Tonight we might watch a movie or go to the mall; but tomorrow when our coworkers ask what we did, we'll say, "Nothing. What about you?" Can you guess their answer?

But God gets even with our ennui. It happened to Fitzgerald, giving him exactly what he wanted—wild success and money, neither of which he could handle. Ironic, isn't it, how slowly life creeps into your rearview mirror, then roars on past, leaving all those major changes in its vaporous wake? Suddenly you're not going to the mall tonight but to Uncle Harry's funeral; you were going to watch *60 Minutes*, but your sister stopped over. Surprise! She's engaged. It's as if God is a preadolescent prankster, greeting us with a celestial joy buzzer to shock us out of the sweet blandness of our lives.

When my wife told me she was pregnant—our first

child—my brain went numb. I was happy, sure, but it was a stunned happiness, like a welcome mallet to the side of the head but without the bruises or headache.

We're going to have a baby...

I was sitting in my underwear eating Teddy Grahams, and all I could think of was how nothing in my life had prepared me for this moment. Despite my watchfulness, despite the small, tight, protective discipline of my routine, I was thrown into another orbit, transformed by wonder.

We're going to have a baby...

It's the wrong time, of course. Our child will join a world that's sliding into chaos; my wife and I can never hope to achieve the security our parents enjoyed. And, by next spring's birth date, our baby may become a citizen of a country at war, with all its attendant splendor and death. If you had to pick a time, this wouldn't be it.

But how many of us choose? Technology has given us the chance at choice, but how many of us are the result of rational thought—or of the unspeakably divine yearning that intercedes for reason?

We're going to have a baby...

This Thanksgiving, somewhere between the turkey and the pumpkin pie, my wife and I will tell our parents the news. There will be hugs and kisses and remarkable clichés, but something more as well: the strange reassurance that it's all worth it—well, worth it enough to try another generation. And if that isn't the voice of God in our genes, right there next to the cranberry sauce, then I'm out of suggestions. Even Scott and Zelda, facing the ever-deepening horror of their twisted lives, found solace in little Scotty, who repaid her parents by keeping the Fitzgerald name alive.

Could we ask for anything more at Thanksgiving? I doubt it. Exhausted by excitement and stuffed full of stuffing, my wife and I will retreat to the corner of the den where the Lions are losing to the Broncos and try to nestle back into the sleepy familiarity of routine. But another voice will whisper to us, barely audible amid the first-quarter stats and reverse-angle replays:

You're going to have a baby. Wake up, wake up, wake up...

Nothing suffers from change as much as taste—or, as Fran Liebowitz once said, "Your right to wear a lime-green polyester suit ends where it meets my eye."

"Fragile Man"

The National Gallery of Art in Washington recently held a retrospective of twentieth-century American art. On the day I toured the East Building, I couldn't help but notice how quickly the visitors—mostly thirtysomething with kids—walked through the exhibit. They never stopped for more than a few seconds at each Rothko, Johns, Warhol, or Pollock. Each baby boomer had a bemused smile, one of irony, as if to ask, "Is this art?"

The exhibit ended on the third floor of the East Building; on the fourth floor was a collection of paintings from Cambridge University. The featured work was *L'Umana fragilita* by seventeenth-century Italian painter Salvator Rosa. The painting depicted a mother, an infant, and Death, who was represented by a winged skeleton. As the mother looked on passively, Death was forcing the baby to scrawl the following words onto a piece of paper: "Conception is sinful, life is suffering, death inevitable." A huge number of the thirtysomething folks stood transfixed by this painting. They were four deep, just staring at it.

It made me wonder. Maybe the novelty of the twentieth century is gone. The newness of discoveries—science, information, even art—has long worn off; everything except numbness. Just think what we have witnessed: man in space, then man on the moon; organ transplants, TV assassinations, TV wars, whole cities and spaceships blowing up in front of our eyes. We have VCRs and microwaves, fuel injectors and personal pagers, satellite feeds and banking machines. When I wrote my last will and testament, I didn't store it in a safety-deposit box but on my computer, complete with backup copies.

All of this in my lifetime. And I'm only thirty years old.

We have lost our sense of awe. Nothing surprises us anymore. Technology doesn't surprise us anymore, only the failure of technology. The question isn't *if* they'll find an AIDS vaccine; the question is why hasn't it been discovered already? What's the holdup? Those who suffer from disease—AIDS, cancer, agoraphobia, whatever—are suspicious of medicine, which has given us cures for polio and dandruff, but can't protect us from deadly viruses, global warming, or things that go bump in the night. We aren't enthralled with scientific advances but confused by the haphazard success. (Overheard at a party: "This environment thing—can't someone *do* something about it?") We wonder when science is going to get its act together so we can all be healthy and happy without the expense of psychotherapy.

If we are disappointed in science and bored by art, is music our salvation? Hardly. Instead, the music charts are full of remakes of old songs, only this time on compact disc. Our idea of risk is reggae. Opera, especially European opera done for the millionth time, represents the limits of our imagination. We have even gone so far as to play old symphonies on original instruments, not trusting our own generation to build violins correctly.

And if not art or science or music, then what? Sports? Even baseball has a green taint now—the artificiality of Astroturf, the reality of money. And if not *baseball,* then *what?*

Recently, while cleaning the attic, I found my notebook from that classic college course, Existentialism. On the back of the notebook was some graffiti I had copied from a men's room at the University of Pittsburgh. It said, "God is dead, (signed) Nietzsche," then, below that, "Nietzsche is dead, (signed) God." And maybe there's some truth in it. Brothers and sisters of my generation are living out a Nietzsche nightmare. The gods who guided them, who vaccinated them against swine flu, who hummed vague, soulless pop lyrics into their ears, who insisted that memorabilia from the television show *M*A*S*H* be installed in the Smithsonian—all of those gods are dead or dying or in trouble with the law.

In fact, the only god who *has* survived is—um—God.

Despite the oppressive cynicism and premature obituaries, religion has persevered. The Romans attacked the Christians, but Christianity made it; the Christians attacked the Muslims, but the Muslims made it; everyone attacked the Jews, but the Jews made it. Religion even survives its periodic self-immolation—it survived the Borgia popes, it survived Jim and Tammy, and it will even survive Khomeini.

"Conception is sinful, life is suffering, death inevitable." With no gods to cling to, these cynical compatriots of mine stood transfixed before this barren summary of their lives. College had prepared them for slings and arrows, etc., but not for painful confrontations like this. Aerobics won't help; self-help books won't help; Larry King won't help. Instead, we'll slog toward the next century, Cuisinarts in tow, left to our own devices. Without an instruction manual or batteries or a sense of history, one wonders what we'll construct for the next generation of doubters.

One wonders if there's anything *left* to doubt. Maybe we've used it all up.

PERHAPS THE MOST LASTING form of change is no change at all: the nagging feeling that you need to resolve something, but you cannot find the will to break out of inertia's grip. So your life wanders on in cruise control, forever changed by that roadblock several miles back. If only you hadn't turned down that offer, or if only you hadn't said X, or if only you *had* said something instead of just standing there...

Most of my roadblocks involve pettiness and selfishness, those great unnamed horses of the Apocalypse. I let my old hurts fester until they're beyond healing, but it's not too late to shout a clichéd warning: it's never too late to say you're sorry.

Only to Find Gideons' Bible

'm sitting in the Altoona Ramada Inn, marking time. Ten years ago this month, Howard put the gun to his head and pulled the trigger. Since then, our little college clique has graduated, gotten married, even held down a job or two. Meanwhile, Howard tries desperately to remember where his car is parked or what day it is or which anticonvulsant to take or which piece of his past he's misplaced yet again in his unfamiliar, rearranged head.

Hotels make me think of Howard. I was in a rundown student dorm in Washington, D.C., when Phil called with the news: "Howard shot himself." Phil had found Howard, alone, in his bedroom, a single trickle of blood from the entrance wound beneath his chin, his bright eyes watching as Phil called the ambulance that would save Howard's life. Phil and Ralph and Gary and Mike would live at the hospital for the next scary days; Phil apologized for not calling earlier: "I haven't been able to speak since Sunday."

Had I believed then, I might have prayed, but I didn't, so God was spared my Catholic *kaddish*. Howard and I hadn't been particularly close, but we shared beer together, occasional rides together, and we shared writing.

Correction: When it came to writing, I stood in Howard's shadow. Everyone did.

Does every college have the one genius, the one raw diamond whose uncut version still staggers even the professors? All our loves were similar—bars, baseball, beat poets—but Howard was the star. We were conceited, unshaven, eclectic, barely tolerable, but Howard was forgiven by his brilliance. We imagined our talent, caught up instead in the clichéd baggage of intellect: cigarettes, white wine, foreign films we didn't understand. Howard meanwhile was huddling in a corner, exchanging addresses with yet another guest lecturer, talking about a poor translation he had read in some quarterly magazine we had never heard of. We forgot our own amateur verse in the face of his sharp, outrageous, unfettered poetry:

> *This is where I am most afraid to die,*
> *here where my soul will leave through my mouth*
> *and sink below the street*
> *through the holes in a manhole cover,*
> *rising only on rainy nights*
> *to dart around in the steam and methane.*
> *I am afraid but I've come looking for something*
> *lost and fragile, something that will*
>   *shatter like crystal*
> *if I drop it, leaving me to gather up the shards*
> *and cut my hands and arms over and over again.*

The crystal finally shattered, I think to myself as I swim laps in the pool at the Altoona Ramada. My eyes sting from too much chlorine, and my head aches from travel, but I am swimming to forget. I'm swimming to forget the pain of seeing Howard in the hospital a few weeks after "the accident," as we so kindly called it. I barely survived the stilted conversation punctuated with pauses, watching his once-bright eyes (now dulled with painkillers) register recognition, but fail to place my name on his lips.

It would be five years before I would see Howard again. The rest of the group made silent pilgrimages to his home; I didn't see the point. I had buried him long ago, but—like the .22 caliber before me—I had failed to kill Howard. He lay quietly in the back of my mind, only to get up and walk around my thoughts when I least expected him. To see Howard again was to see a corpse—or worse, because Howard's corpse lacked Howard's voice. His speech was as unsteady as his gait, and his rambling sentences rarely found their point, and the Pirates game we were watching suddenly became a Penguins game in the twisted fuse box of Howard's mind.

Back in my room, unable to sleep, unable to endure a rerun of SportsCenter, I pick up a Gideons' Bible. Someone has left the marker on the Book of Samuel. As his child lays dying, David fasts and prays; when the child dies, David anoints himself and goes forth. "You fasted and wept for the child while it was alive," his servants say, "but when the child died, you arose and ate food."

> David said, "While the child was still alive, I fasted and wept; for I said, 'Who knows whether the Lord will be gracious to me, that the child may live?' But now he is dead; why should I fast? Can I bring him back again? I shall go to him, but he will not return to me."

In college, I didn't believe in God, so God was spared my *kaddish*. But in ten years, I have never prayed for Howard. I realize now, as I watch the jousting headlights on Route 22, that anger's sword had speared the side of my past, and out came only bile. I could forgive Howard a temporary lapse in sanity; I could forgive him the off-center imagination which hounded him to try the solace of suicide; I could even forgive the unfair theft of that sheer promise, that Howard-to-be. But I am too selfish, too pathetically rigid, to accept him as he is now.

I could rejoice in his new accomplishments, the little joys of a simplified life, the way we cheer the small victories of a stroke victim or another day of sobriety for a recovering alcoholic. I *could*, but no. David could anoint his sorrow and move on; I am too angry, too much a sinner of wistfulness, so my unburied past rots like bad fruit in the jowls of my memory.

In this small sanctuary in Altoona, among the twin beds and paper-wrapped cups and little bottles of shampoo and conditioner, I offer my overdue prayer for Howard in the urgent language of my deepest memory:

Mea culpa, Howard, mea maxima culpa.

I SPENT MANY WEEKENDS as a teenager on the shores of the Youghiogheny River. There was one rock (though we called it a cliff) that stretched out into a calm, deep pool. On the first visit every summer, we had to work up enough guts to rebaptize ourselves by jumping from that rock perch fifteen feet above the river. Each of us, in turn, required cajoling to take that first step—and when we felt the ice-cold Yough embrace us, we all had the same thought: We tamed nature.

But not really, not really. We had never conquered the cliffs, only survived them. In those first few moments after you leave the safety of the rock, you think about dying—if you survive, it's only a tie. The cliffs will never be conquered because there will always be higher cliffs, and the best you can ever hope for is a draw.

So much for taming nature. Change often requires a change in attitude, of knowing one's limits—as a person or as a species.

Evolution, Genesis, and Earth Day

It's ironic that one of the turning points in Science—capital S—was an apple. One fell from a tree, the story goes, and Isaac Newton gave us the Theory of Gravity.

Einstein later turned Newton's theory on its ear, but that's no matter—just a little skirmish in the scientific family. The ancient Greeks believed that thunder and lightning were the sounds of the gods battling; our modern-day gods—those sullen men and women of science in their sullen white smocks—confine their battles to civilly obscure scientific journals.

Now a member of that deity has written a book which may expose this family for what it is: mortal. Harvard paleontologist Stephen Jay Gould's *Wonderful Life* suggests that a key tenet of evolution, the ascent of man, wasn't really an "ascent" at all—just dumb luck.

After examining the 570-million-year-old fossil record at the Burgess Shale quarry in western Canada, Gould found no evidence that the species who survived are any better than the species who didn't. One species wasn't "superior" to the others nor more "adaptable"; some species died off for inexplicable reasons—maybe comets, maybe viruses, maybe kismet—but *not* inferiority. Humanity's survival, Gould guesses, is nothing more than a series of outrageously fortuitous events, a combination of the right place, the right time, and pure chance. That loaded word, *evolution*, is survival of the luckiest, not the fittest.

But this isn't just another family squabble between scientific in-laws. It's as if the family has discovered that Uncle Harry is a cockroach, and *we're* Uncle Harry. Whatever happened to our reigning position on the planet, our divine rule? We tamed the place, we wrote the rules, we *must* be the pedigrees, the superior stock. After all, evolution is *our* damn theory. You don't see whales or sequoias teaching at Harvard, do ya?

Which proves that the creationists were right all along. No, *not* the creationists who think we were magically made in seven days. I mean Genesis. God gave us paradise but with one caveat: don't nab an apple from the tree of knowledge. But did we listen? Nope. We were beguiled by a smooth-talking snake who made us think that one bite would make us rulers of the universe, even as smart as What's-His-Countenance with the beard.

So we were taught a lesson. And you would have thought we'd have learned the first time; but no—here we are again, ruining our Eden with bad chemicals, bad decisions, and myopia. Darwin has the right facts, but Genesis has the better metaphor. It's not enough to know who your ancestors are—you're supposed to learn from their mistakes.

Maybe the fundamentalists are right. We *should* teach Genesis right alongside evolution. There's no doubt that Darwin was right, but Darwin doesn't teach us what "survival" really means. Maybe the story of the Fall will teach our youth about the consequences of pride: that we aren't rulers of this planet but part of it; that the rain forests and oceans and resources may one day give up fighting us for their fair share, and we'll be banished—for a second time—from paradise.

It's hard to imagine we'll get a third chance...and harder to imagine that we deserve one.

SURPRISE! This is *not* another homily about crass commercialism ruining the holidays. It is, however, about insecurity, dread, and last-minute shopping—the Thirteenth, Fourteenth, and Fifteenth Days of Christmas. Despite cheerful encouragement about the "Spirit of the Season," no normal person over the age of seventeen looks forward to this most holy of days.

Then, like magic, every Who down in Who-ville, the tall and the small, start singing...

The Holidays
at Thirty-One

Christmas is an old girlfriend calling. Your wife has left a message:

> *Mary C. called.*
> *She'll call again later.*

You examine your spouse's handwriting, looking for signs of indignation or (worse) indifference. She betrays nothing—-her casualness in direct contrast to your black mood. Then the phone rings, and you hear your girlfriend's voice again, the rasp from too many Marlboros, a habit she claims to have kicked. She asks how you've been, your plans for the holidays, even asks about your wife. Then the big one: *I'll be in town next week. Why don't we get together?* And you feel trapped, reluctant to say yes, unwilling to say no. She takes your silence for acquiescence, and here you are again—another visitor from your past.

She says she has a gift for you.

"How thoughtful," you lie.

You feel ridiculous as you walk through the intervening days, unable to forget the impending "date." Other people seem preoccupied as well, everyone's face etched in dread. You can't believe this is happening again. It seems like just a few months ago, but it was much longer than that.

You don't want to shop for a gift, but you must. Your wife offers to "pick up something" for you—again, that baffling casualness—but you decline. You wander through the crowded stores, despising the holiday ads and come-ons, angrier than ever. A gift counter promises a free makeup case with every ten-dollar purchase "for that special someone." You feel like torching the place, watching all the green and red decorations turn black and curl.

Back at home, unable to sleep, you stare at late-night television. Every commercial features smiling families gathered together—hugs and kisses all the way around. You wonder if these people went shopping like you did. You wonder what happened to *their* message pad, the one that reads, *Mary C. called. She'll call again later.*

As always, dread makes time fly, and you're caught unprepared. You do last-minute shopping, finally selecting a perfectly inadequate scarf, and then run home to get dressed.

It's getting ready that's worst of all—not because you don't enjoy it, but because you do. It's the thrill of special clothes, of looking just right, of actually looking forward to this terrible night. *I'm too old for this,* you think. You feel stupid and sheepish around your wife.

"How did I get roped into this?" you ask her, a little too plaintive.

"Oh, enjoy yourself," she says, smiling, relaxed, "this is supposed to be fun." Her cheerful, inexplicable mood is finally broken when you spill shoe polish on the new carpet in the hallway.

Driving to the restaurant, you feel like a kid again, as if you managed to borrow Dad's car just to make an impression. You check your hair in the rearview mirror and check your breath for the millionth time. You cannot believe how excited you feel and wonder—also for the millionth time—why you've never grown up. *I'm not a kid,* you think to yourself, *I shouldn't feel this way,* all the while smoothing the stubborn wrinkles out of your new tie.

"There'll be a short wait," the maître d' says, as if your heart can stand one more delay. You hesitate at the bar but reconsider—you're not pretty when you drink.

Then you see her waving hand. Your optometrist has been talking bifocals, but you see her as clearly as the day you first met. How young you both were! Like magic, the dread and excitement disappear. You walk over to her, smiling, and kiss her smack on the lips, without restraint now, because it'll be okay. Everything will be okay. You'll eat, you'll talk, you'll remember. She'll give you her gift—

a tie exactly like the one you're wearing, and you'll both laugh. She'll praise your token scarf, and you'll thank her for her kindness. When it's over, you'll say your long good-byes and go back to your wife, the best part of all. You'll think how wonderful Mary C. is, and how happy you are you married your wife.

On the drive home, between the red lights and memories, you wonder why you dreaded this night. You know the truth without admitting it: that by seeing her again you'd see what you had lost—not her, but that part of yourself, your past, your youth, your first blush of love. You had thought—*hoped*—that you had outgrown such nostalgia but realize now how wonderful it all is: a sad, comic opera, the only life you know, leading you past the side streets and poorly marked detours, taking you home. And it's *not* your Dad's car, it's *your* car, and it runs pretty well, despite the high mileage.

At home, your wife asks, "How did it go?" and you know right away that she knew all along. And it's like seeing *her* for the first time again—not the amphetamine of adolescent craving, but the bone-deep realization. She is me. We is us. She is my mirror, my bifocal vision, my imperfect skin. You cannot believe how lucky you are, how happy to be a grownup. *This* life, right now.

Before you go to bed, you pen a quick thank-you to your old girlfriend, then stub your little toe as you search for a stamp in the dark. It's a short, stupid note, but you want it to go out in the morning mail:

Merry Christmas, Mary C.
Will you be in town next year?

FATHER MATTHEW FOX was once asked if he thought God was a pessimist. "No," Fox said, "I think she enjoys herself."

It's a stand-up line that's meant to draw a laugh, but I'm not so sure about God's sense of humor. It's not the kind of humor I'd call funny as much as ironic: the dog on three legs who falls over when he wets on the fire hydrant; the tone-deaf child born to musically gifted parents; the car that starts up every morning for work but fails miserably on weekends.

And then there's the cruel jokes—war, caste, poverty, tyranny, disease. God gives us wine, for instance, the fruit of the bountiful harvest—and gives us the burden of alcoholism running through our genes like a freight train without brakes. We do our best to ignore the addicts in our midst, trying to pretend we don't know them, that we're not related to them, that they're not us.

If God is testing us, then at least we know the question: It's hard to be a saint in the city, ain't it?

A Wound to Fit the Bandage

"Everyone in seminary wanted to be a saint," recalls the former Father William "Jay" Geisler, thirty-four, speaking to a group of recovering addicts at a weekly meeting in the North Hills section of Pittsburgh.

"So did I—until I found out how much saints *suffered*. I decided I'd rather drink."

Suffering, recovery, setbacks—Jay Geisler's life intersects these themes again and again. "Before I became a priest, I was a fourth-generation steelworker," Geisler says. "Drinking is like a rite of manhood."

The room is full of recovering addicts, a cross section of rich and poor, black and white, those hooked on heroin and those hooked on Heineken. Like most of those present, Geisler started drinking and smoking pot in high school, "where I always felt outside the group, like everybody's second-best friend. So I'd drink to fit in—a six-pack at a time. A six-pack for openers! I was *impressive*."

Always a top student, Geisler attended a Catholic college, ran for class president on the "Sin" ticket, and stepped up his addiction. "We'd have smoke-a-thons and keggers in the Blessed Virgin's grotto, because it was the prettiest place on campus." He graduated with a history degree and few prospects for a job, so he returned to his family's employer for more than four decades, LTV Steel's Aliquippa Works.

"I wore my mill greens with a dress shirt, a biker's wallet and a plastic pocket protector," Geisler remembers. "I was something between a nerd and a wimp."

He was also a champion drinker, discovering a fondness for boilermakers. "Once I drank for five hours, then wrecked my car into St. Boniface Church on the North Side. When I came to, I was looking at the church entrance. *Oh my God,* I thought, *I went and killed myself.* Then I noticed the church doors were locked. *Great,* I thought, *I died and went to hell.*"

Geisler's life began to turn around when he met "a good Catholic girl" who persuaded him to return to church. "When I left her place one night, I was going to light up my ritual evening joint, and I thought, *What am I doing? I've got a good job, a nice car, a wonderful girlfriend, a nice life. Why do I smoke so much?* So I didn't."

The next day, his girlfriend was dead, a heart attack at nineteen. "I promised to stop doing drugs from that moment on," he said. But it wasn't a promise he kept, nor did he quit drinking. He was late for her funeral because he stopped at a liquor store to buy a bottle of Yukon Jack. "When I hurt, I drank. When I felt good, I drank. When I didn't know how I felt, I drank."

Her death sent Geisler into an extended period of soul-searching, seeking direction in his life. He finally narrowed his choices to the military or the seminary. "That's typical of me," Geisler says. "Didn't know whether to bomb them or bless them."

The seminary responded first, and Geisler found himself "in a classroom of seriously religious types frantically scribbling notes—and there I was wearing a Proud to be a Steelworker T-shirt and biker's boots." Geisler found his niche as head of the "renovation committee," which meant he got keys to the campus pub. "Our first project was renovating the pub. So was our second."

He become well-known in the seminary. On one retreat, he shaved his head and grew a Fu Manchu mustache. "Sort of Kung Fu spirituality," he remembers. He traveled through Europe, vowing that if he "made it through the Continent without being with a woman, it was a sign from God that I should really be ordained." He did make it, though not without smuggling drugs and drinking heavily. All during seminary, Geisler earned good grades and several academic awards. "I thought I was doing good," he recalls, and the diocese apparently agreed, honoring Geisler's request to be assigned to a steel-town parish—Aliquippa's St. Titus Church.

He didn't make friends immediately, not even with fellow priests. "The three priests (at St. Titus) represented the spectrum of the Church: the pastor was Vatican I, the associate pastor was Vatican II, and I was Vatican III. I was asking questions like 'Should we baptize extraterrestrials?'" But he was popular with the gang who frequented a motorcycle bar in "the 'Quip.'" "So there I was, the night before I turned thirty, in a fight with one of the patrons. I had him in a full nelson, pinned against the bar, ready to beat the hell out of him." At six-feet-three, two hundred twenty-five pounds, Geisler can make such boasts. "Then I thought of the headlines: 'Priest Kills Biker in Bar.' So I looked up and thought, *God, Jesus started his ministry at thirty—help me, too.*"

That was four years ago. With the exception of one relapse, he hasn't touched a drink since. Geisler finishes his speech to the North Hills recovery group by saying, "Sometimes I think I'm the next president, and sometimes I think I'm full of it. I wish one of those little old ladies in the parish would have come up to me just once and said, 'Jay, you are full of it.' I would have been a lot better off."

The speech is part Geisler's latest ministry: working with alcoholics and addicts as part of St. Francis Hospital's outreach program in Pittsburgh. But Geisler's special mission is the homeless. He founded the Pittsburgh Recovery Center, a walk-in rehabilitation satellite of St. Francis' drug-and-alcohol program. The center's Penn Avenue location is designed to attract the homeless and indigent addicts who frequent the saddest sections of downtown Pittsburgh. Although the center brings in a steady street trade, Geisler also visits addicted homeless on their turf: the city's shelters.

On this particular day, Geisler is talking to "Bill," a forty-six-year-old former computer operator, at the Good Samaritan Shelter. "I don't qualify for welfare anymore," he tells Geisler. "I cheated on two checks in 1985, and they won't let me have any more."

"Were you using then?" Geisler asks.

"Of course I was."

"Then appeal it," Geisler says. "Tell them you were using when it happened and you're in recovery now. Tell them that during your appeal."

Bill turns away; it's hard to tell if he believes Geisler or not.

"It's depressing living here, you know," he says to me (a "civilian," in recovery parlance). "I used to work with computers. I went to New York University. But now I can't even go out on the streets. I wasn't only a user, I was very active."

"You mean you hustled," Geisler interjects.

"Not exactly."

"Then you dealt?"

"Well, let's just say I was very active," Bill says. "How I used would depend on how I made money. If I earned it from a good job, I wouldn't spend it. But if it was from drugs, I'd use. I didn't feel good about how I got it.

Besides, if I fenced, say, three balloons [dealt three containers of heroin], the people I'd deal with would say, 'Okay, you and me.' And I'd have to do some; otherwise they'd get suspicious. It was a friendship thing, I guess, or it was supposed to be...."

"Still clean?" Geisler asks.

"Thirty days," Bill says. Geisler stares at him. "Swear to God," Bill says, raising his right hand.

"Then good for you." ("The problem in dealing with addicts who are using," Geisler tells me later, "is that every time they move their lips they lie.")

Before leaving, Bill says to me, "Hope is just a word to me, but it's all I got." Everything he owns is in a locker at the Greyhound Bus terminal, and he had lost the key while he was drinking. "By now, they've probably put it all in storage," he says, "and I don't have the money to get it out." Yesterday he spent his last dollar buying a get-well card for his girlfriend, who has just checked into St. Francis' detox unit.

It was Easter Sunday, 1988, when Jay Geisler celebrated his last Mass as a Roman Catholic priest. After an eighteen-month leave of absence from St. Titus parish, Geisler officially resigned from the priesthood. Leaving the Church "was one of the most difficult decisions of my life," Geisler says. "I was raised Catholic. I *am* Catholic. I still want to serve God, though I'm not sure where he's leading me." Geisler admits his own priestly celibacy was not without trial, "but I can't believe he wanted me to be alone all my life."

Not everyone was sorry to see him leave. "I'm sure not everyone supported Jay. I'm not sure every *priest* supported Jay. But I know he had his supporters. I know he had support down at St. Titus," says the Rev. Donald McIlvane of Presentation Catholic Church in neighboring Midland, Pennsylvania. McIlvane, like Geisler, has been criticized for his social activism, which dates back two decades. "It's a tough life, but it doesn't always come to this."

In his resignation letter to his bishop, Geisler argued that several key issues drove him from the Church: birth control, mandatory celibacy, annulments rather than divorce, the ban on women priests, and closed communion (only Roman Catholics can receive communion at Catholic Mass; other denominations allow any baptized Christian to the altar). "Since seminary, I have given silent assent to these issues," Geisler told Wuerl, "but I believe I can do this no longer after seeing them made concrete in practical pastoral ministry."

Geisler calls these five issues "a crisis brewing" in the Church. ("It's only five theses," Geisler says. "Luther had ninety-five.") But McIlvane and others disagree with the "crisis" label. "These questions are vital, but they've been topics in the Church for some time now," McIlvane says. "For example, some would say that the contraception issue has come and gone for the American Catholic Church. People have made up their own minds." Longtime activist Msgr. Charles Owen Rice concurs: "We didn't lose people because we weren't liberal enough; we lost older Catholics because we weren't *conservative* enough, and we lost younger Catholics because—well, because young people don't seem to believe in *anything* anymore."

"I know Jay is concerned about the celibacy issue," says the Rev. David L. Kinsey, head of Episcopal Service Ministries, who help to fund the Recovery Center. "But I wonder if at least part of his decision to join the priesthood was in reaction to his girlfriend's death. When people lose a partner, there's a reaction, sometimes an impulsive one. I'm not questioning his faith—he's very committed—but I wonder if he reacted by joining the seminary, then thought later about all of the consequences."

And that seems to be the heart of the matter—not an abstract question of Church politics or social policy, but a personal question of intimacy. After all, I ask Geisler, "why the sudden change?" Didn't he know all this before he entered the Catholic priesthood?

"Yes," he says, quietly. "In the past three years, I've changed my vocation, my job, my entire life. I'm thirty-four years old and living with my parents. And I can't blame anyone or complain about how people have treated me. The diocese has been understanding. And St. Francis had a lot of courage hiring a priest who was on a leave of absence. But it's still a struggle. One thing they teach you in recovery is to be honest with yourself. I guess I'm finding out exactly what that means."

Dana Gold, who works closely with Geisler as head of the Good Samaritan Shelter, offers a different perspective: "Jay feels comfortable working with needy people, probably because of his own experience of being broken. But he's also chosen—or has been called—to work with addicts because he understands them. We all minister out of our own brokenness; sometimes you look for a wound to fit the bandage."

"THOSE WHO BELIEVE that they believe in God," wrote Spanish philosopher Miguel de Unamuno, "but believe without passion in their hearts, without anguish in their mind, without uncertainty, without doubt, without an element of despair even in their consolation, believe only in the God idea, not in God himself."

Death Knows the Repo Man

This is a story about my friend Lauren, who is dying of leukemia, and an Audi 4000S.

No generation has mortgaged so much, and done it so quickly, as the present generation. Consumerism and borrowed money are at all-time highs. Status standards have improved from the comfortable to the outrageous: BMWs, one-hundred-dollar haircuts, designer underwear. Young, successful Americans now face the difficult choices of power windows versus heated seats or of how many skylights in their newly built homes. They cannot afford either, but banks offer generous terms and extended credit. Who cares about a double-digit car loan when you have six years to pay?

America's passion for excess has poisoned the world. Russian youth rock to Billy Joel in seventy-dollar black-market Levi's; South American countries take out loans to pay interest on previous loans. Brazil stopped paying its creditors and isn't allowed to borrow again. Some penalty—I say good for Brazil.

Brazil will be the first of many to default—and not just some faraway country but your cousin Fred and his shiny new wife Muffin. They just bought a condo in Shadyside ("It's a little pricey but close to everything," Muffy says) and also an Audi 4000S—"with overdrive," Fred tells you, "so it'll really save on gas." Sure it will. When bad times come—as they surely must—Fred will be sleeping in their gas-efficient Audi with a loaded gun, fending off the repossession agent. Banks were kind to Brazil by comparison; they taught Brazil how to live without credit and never once sent a repo man.

I'm not sure Fred and Muffin will ever learn. Money has been their entire, albeit short, lives. All they know is work, good restaurants, VCRs, and aerobics. Fred's idea of spirituality is Bruce Springsteen's lyrics, many of which contain biblical references. Muffy once signed a petition to protect the whales, and calls herself an environmentalist. They give twenty dollars to CARE each Christmas, then take a two-hundred-dollar write-off on their taxes. Their most heartfelt discussions revolve around separate versus joint bank accounts. They've talked about kids but don't think they can afford it now—neither could give up their job. Late at night, too tired to make love, they feel lonely and unfulfilled; each secretly blames the other for the time slipping by.

Time *is* slipping by—Lauren couldn't agree more. "Take out all the loans you can get because you can't tell what might happen. Live for the present," she would say—

because the present is all Lauren has. Money has failed her. Expensive chemotherapy followed by more expensive bone-marrow transplants, and she has nothing to show for her pain but mottled skin and a few wisps of hair. She's twenty-eight years old and won't see thirty. In the past year, she has reconciled herself to Death, who sits in her hospital room with his feet propped up on her nightstand, eating boxed candy and watching reruns.

Lauren says they've talked. Death, she says, is impatient.

When Lauren talks like that, I want to run out of her hospital room, back to my new, air-conditioned car and its new-car smell. Lauren's room smells like Death's aftershave—a mixture of disease and loss, the thick yellow solution that drips into the darkness of Lauren's body, a body that has betrayed her.

I want to sit in Lauren's room with a loaded rifle and hold off Death forever. But Lauren says no. "I've tried it already," she shrugs.

I've begun to pray again.

And this is my prayer: to tell Muffy and Fred to leave the Audi at home and walk to the church or temple of their choice. If Fred doesn't believe or if Muffy isn't sure, then pray for me instead, because I'm scared. My life is bankrupt, and Death knows the repo man.

–For Lisa M.

TWO MONTHS BEFORE THIS ESSAY first appeared in print, I marched against a Klu Klux Klan rally in Washington County, Pennsylvania, where a Klansman told me, "Only three kinds of people don't like the Klan—niggers, nigger lovers, Jews, and queers." He couldn't count very well, but he was inspirational enough to sign up three new members, including a nine-year-old boy.

As we drove away from the rally, I said to my friend, "It's not often that you get to feel this righteous." My friend replied, "It's not often this simple. It's hardly ever clear-cut."

He's right, of course. It's a lot easier to march against the Klan than it is to acknowledge our own biases, our own blindness. And change—*real change*—won't happen until we snuff out the burning crosses that light our landscapes like false gods. Such is the price of democracy: it depends on us.

Monongahela Burning

Last January, as I crossed the bridge from Route 88 to Route 136 in Monongahela, Pennsylvania, I noticed what looked like a cross lit with Christmas lights—

gold and blue lights shimmering against the dark hillside. I thought it was a little late for Christmas decorations, and a cross seemed inappropriate for the season anyway. I also noticed how big the cross was. Although distance skewed my perception, it seemed at least twenty feet tall. From its perch halfway up the hill, the cross looked out over the City of Monongahela. It occurred to me that the cross might belong to an overzealous fundamentalist, who perhaps kept up this garish display year round.

As I drove further across the bridge, though, the lights kept wavering and changing, and I realized that they weren't lights at all, but flames.

The cross was on fire—there was a cross burning in Monongahela.

Instead of turning right toward Route 51, I turned left to get a better look. I couldn't believe what I was seeing. Maybe it was a telephone pole on fire or someone burning trash that happened to take this miraculous shape. But there was no mistaking it—it was a cross, completely engulfed, probably soaked in kerosene to make it burn evenly.

I parked my car so I faced the cross. I had an Instamatic with me and fumbled for the flashcube in the glove compartment. I travel this road a lot, and it's usually empty. On this particular night, though, it was crowded with cars. Across from me was a road that ran up the hill toward the cross. Perhaps it was just coincidence, but in the short time I was there, half a dozen cars came down that hill. The last car, a Chevy, stopped, its headlights trained on me.

The lights were blinding, making my search for the

flashcube even more difficult. At first, I thought the car was waiting to turn; then I realized traffic had stopped. Either the two guys in the Chevy were lost, or they were watching me.

I found the flashcube and attached it to my camera. Then I started the car, as if I were leaving. The Chevy finally made its turn. I waited, then took my picture. I knew it would be blurry if it came out at all, but I wanted some proof—*proof*—of what I had seen. (The picture, of course, didn't turn out.)

I was going to take another picture, but the Chevy had stopped and was turning around. I pulled onto 136 and passed them, discovering along the way that my Mazda's reported top speed of 81 mph was thankfully underrated.

I didn't slow down until I reached a pay phone on Route 51. I kept thinking that it was all a mistake—maybe it *was* a telephone pole, and maybe the guys in the Chevy *were* lost. But nothing worked. Even if it were a sick prank, I knew what I had seen. I don't know why I called the police—perhaps I just wanted to talk to someone who could do something.

"Monongahela police."

"Is, um, is there something on fire across from the hospital?"

"Yep."

"It looks like a cross."

"That's what it is."

I was stunned—not by what he said but by his casual voice.

"Does this happen a lot?"

"I hope not. I hope it's not the start of something."

Then, maybe sensing how I felt, he added, "There was no one up there." That meant they had checked, but I didn't feel any better.

I knew there were newspapers in the Mon Valley, but I didn't know their names, so I called the Associated Press.

"I think I saw a cross burning in Monongahela."

"You probably did."

Again the casualness, as if it were another Elvis sighting.

"You mean you hear about this stuff often?"

"Often enough."

I was so surprised, I called him back. "How often is often?"

"I don't know, maybe every couple months."

Every couple months—it wasn't even *news* anymore.

A lot of things went through my mind during the drive home. I remember stories my mother told me about the KKK in central Pennsylvania and how they had frightened her. I asked her why she was scared—after all, we weren't black.

"They hate everyone who isn't like them," she said. "We're Catholic—that's one of the reasons they burn a cross: it looks like a crucifix."

"But why do they burn *anything*?" I asked. My mother did not have an answer.

And here I was, two decades older but none wiser, making a fool of myself to the police and press. I had actually imagined my blurry little snapshot splashed across the pages of the *Press* and the *Post-Gazette*, with hammerhead headlines and eyewitness interviews. But it wasn't news. It happens too often to be news—well, "often enough."

There's much of this story that still bothers me. My alarming naivete, the triumph of fear, the indifference bordering on tolerance. But recently I've been thinking about the power each of us possesses. Think of it: as long as you have the correct permits, it's perfectly legal to burn a cross. Last November, the KKK held a perfectly legal cross-burning in Washington County; the cross was set alight after a fiery speech by a nine-year-old Klansman.

And if my children ever ask, "Why is it legal to burn a cross?" I will have an answer. I will tell them that some people are fooled by freedom's double edge, thinking they can outlaw bad taste and ugly thoughts but retain their *own* rights. They see what they *want* to see, instead of what is really there. Some people mistake a burning cross for Christmas lights, and you can only hope that they will learn to tell the difference.

FEW CHANGES CAUSE such exquisite ambivalence as children. One day you're laying odds on the little tyke's chances at the Nobel peace prize; the next day you're calling the Child Abuse Hotline, confessing a fantasy about drop-kicking Johnny into the next zip code. And this agony/ecstasy starts from the moment of conception—a moment of unbridled passion followed immediately by bridled doubt.

For all of those parents who love their children without reservation and who manage to get through the day without swearing and who wouldn't *think* of using a pacifier that had fallen on the floor—this essay isn't for you. It's for the rest of us, who, like Joseph, accept parenthood with a mixture of confusion and joy, and whose lives are made richer by exactly these extremes.

Faith

It's one in the morning—well, twelve fifty-six, but who's counting?—and Faith wants to be held and rocked. Our daughter is less than two months old, and already sleep has become my god. I worship it, I praise it, I give it glory. If it asked for burnt offerings, I would gladly make ready the altar.

"C'mon, Faith," I whisper, "time for bed. Aren't you tired?" She looks at me with those enormous blue startled eyes. She's wide awake. I walk and rock some more, thinking of myself asleep at my desk tomorrow morning.

Faith is our first child, and you can explain a first child. You didn't know any better. Or you didn't know what to expect. Or you didn't know where children came from. Or cousin Gertrude had one and you thought it was cute. Or it just seemed like the thing to want.

Before Faith, my wife and I talked about two or three kids, but we don't talk like that anymore. (Our conversations are strictly physiological: Did she do big potty? Does that barf look okay to you?) But most families have more than one child, and how to explain that? "After a year of night feedings, sore nipples, baby throw up, diaper pails, colic, leaking breasts, diaper rash, a ruined wardrobe, and $4,672 on our Toys Я Us charge card—oh, and did I mention sleeplessness?—we've decided to have another child."

Right. Now let these nice boys hold you down while I pump you full of industrial-strength Thorazine before it's too late. I mean, isn't wanting another child a leading symptom of sleep deprivation? Surely it's a sign of an unfit parent.

> *1:07 a.m.: C'mon, Faith, go to sleep. I'll pay you a dollar...okay, ten dollars! A sawbuck if you'll just close your eyes...*

Night feedings also mean watching CNN in your underwear, trying to remember what the outside world is like. (Is Bush still president?) But instead it fuels your raging apprehensions. Suddenly, news reports of drive-by shootings, natural disasters, and outrageous misfortune are no longer arbitrary. Susan Rook is winking at me: *Listen up, Mark,* she's saying, *nothing is safe.*

I switch to the Weather Channel, only to find electrical storms headed east. The chances of lightning striking are—what? one in ten thousand? I turn off the television anyway, just in case a stray bolt strikes the cable and barrels into my living room, into Faith's ear.

Well, it *could* happen.

> *1:33 a.m.: Listen, Faith, I don't want to mention any names, but somebody's in trouble with his boss tomorrow unless you go to sleep...*

Nothing makes you more paranoid than parenthood. Every noise in the night is the harbinger of disaster. A cough means the croup; flies bear the bubonic plague. Suspicion makes you double-check labels and warranties. Is your car seat on the recall list? Is the formula expired? I've joined the ranks of the Terminally Suspicious. We arm ourselves with deadbolt locks and distrust. Is that a broken-down motorist at the door, or the Boston Strangler? Even my education is suspect. I realize now what the nuns didn't teach me: evil rules the world, not good. War, revolution, oppression—these are the subheads of history. Was it Hitler who made the earth shake, or Mother Teresa? (Forty years among the untouchables and she gets the Nobel prize; forty minutes across the Oder River and he gets Poland. I wonder who will command a bigger chunk of Faith's history books?)

> *1:47 a.m.: How 'bout if I sing you to sleep? Let's see—I don't know any lullabies...*

He's a hairy-handed gent who ran amok in Kent
Lately he's been overheard in Mayfair
Better stay away from him—he'll rip
  your lungs out, Jim!
Oh, I'd like to meet his tailor.
Aaahh-ooooo! Werewolves of London...

Why are you crying? Okay, so you don't like
Warren Zevon...

Finally, she falls asleep on my shoulder. I put her down—oh, so gently—on her tummy, then rock the cradle until I'm sure she won't awaken when I creep out of the room. But I don't creep out. Funny—all that struggle to get her down, and now I don't want to leave. Her sleep, so instantly deep, seems like the sleep of ages, like the peace one prays for in church.

And I start thinking that my daughter might like a sibling. Is it Faith's selfishness that keeps my wife and I from talking about another child, or our own? Wouldn't she like a partner to share her visions, her secret discoveries? Won't she need a blood friend to confide in, to share stories about her mighty strange parents?

And I think that maybe it's God winking at me, not Susan Rook: God the optimist, who can't fathom our continued self-subversion yet refuses to give up. If evil men change history, it's only because they overcome the inertia of optimism that moves us all quietly forward each day. Perhaps, amid our petty destructive childishness, is also the childlike quality of hope that makes us foolishly believe in tomorrow.

Faith rustles as if she's waking, then drops asleep again. I creep out on all fours, pulling the door half shut behind me. I crawl in next to my wife (it'll be her turn at five a.m.) and realize that the two of us have passed the primary test for bearing a second child.

First, we had Faith.

SOME OF WHAT FOLLOWS never happened: I never had a grandfather in the war, never knew Mrs. Aiello, and never had to worry about registering. But there really is a George Dickel whiskey, there really is an Argonne Forest, and there really is a burden to one's own personal history—as well as the shared burden of our violent past. To change this spiral of madness means understanding the victims of war—not those who died, but those who remain behind.

Autumn 1981

M rs. Aiello waddles across the street toward me in a lavender housecoat and fuzzy yellow slippers with nylon anklets. Despite the sun, she is wearing a rain hat to hide the random hair rollers pinned unevenly about her head. The rain hat is transparent and covers nothing. Mrs. Aiello is bringing yet another pot of beef broth.

I stop raking and swab my forehead. I am already

sweating with this light exercise—eighteen and out of shape. I smile at Mrs. Aiello and say, "Good afternoon."

"You should be watching the baseball game," she says. (It is November—baseball has been over for nearly a month.) "Here, give this to your mother."

I fold my work gloves and use them as potholders: (Mrs. Aiello must have fireproof fingers.) "Thanks, Mrs. A.," I tell her. "Do you need someone to rake your leaves?"

"Maybe," she says, "if my son doesn't get to it first." In the language of our neighborhood, there is a translation: *I need someone to rake the leaves, but I don't know how to ask for help.*

"Well, thanks again for the broth, Mrs. Aiello. Your soup is always something special." Mrs. Aiello turns, smiling and shaking her head. "Your mother is lucky," she calls over her shoulder, "to have a boy like you."

I take the pot into the house. It is uncomfortable when she talks like that. Inside, my mother and father are drinking their afternoon coffee. I set the soup on the counter.

"Not again," my father says.

"Oh, yes," I say.

Without a word my mother rises to fish out a Tupperware canister big enough to hold this half-gallon of stock. She'll freeze at least a quart; we'll have it again sometime this week. My father and I smile at each other.

"How was she dressed?" he asks.

"Now, Bill..." my mother starts, but stops.

"Purple housecoat," I tell him, "with torn pockets. These fuzzy yellow scuffies on her feet—looked like bald tennis balls. And pink curlers (my father is laughing now) neatly tucked inside a clear plastic rain cap. I think she's going on a date or something."

"Now that's enough," my mother says, and my father and I both know to shut up. He turns to his wife for a second but says nothing—knows, in fact, she is right to stop our humor.

"I'm going to head out," my father says. "Do you need a trash bag?"

"Couple," I say. "It's heavier this year, or quicker. All the leaves seem to fall right into our yard."

"Figures," he says. I have inherited his fatalism. My father shrugs on his pea coat from the Navy and goes outside. The kitchen is quiet for a while.

"Sorry," I say finally.

"Did you talk to your guidance counselor yet?" she asks, ladling the broth into the plastic container. She is a master at changing subjects.

"You mean about registering?"

She nods.

"No," I say, "not yet." It's a reply meant to keep her at bay, and it works—my mother looks out the window as she burps the Tupperware cover.

"I wonder if Ava needs any help?" she asks, staring across the street.

"I asked her if she needed help with the raking," I say quickly, thankful for the chance to redeem myself. "She said no, but I think she does. She said her son would do it."

My mother turns abruptly from the window and becomes overly involved with the soup stock and coffee cups. I shouldn't have said anything, but now it's too late.

"Well," I offer quietly, "I better get back to it."

"All right," she says. Before I'm gone she calls, "Will you ask him on Monday? About the registering?"

"Sure," I say, and I'm out the door.

On her porch, Mrs. Aiello drapes a throw rug over the railing and beats it with a long stick. As I rake, I remember another scene on the Aiello porch eight years ago.

Mrs. Aiello was the greatest den mother ever. We'd have candy apples at our meetings, and she'd make every medal earned feel somehow special—even the bobcat badge. *Do twenty push-ups. Twenty sit-ups. Make something out of Balsa wood. Report your activities to your den leader.* We won the Halloween contest twice and the jamboree rally once. In the two years she was den mother, I actually wore my yellow handkerchief and regulation cap.

She was a black-lung widow; her only son, Tony, eleven years my senior, had been an Eagle Scout. He was a clean-cut kid, second-string linebacker on a conference champion. My Dad said Tony was the only paper boy who folded the newspaper twice—perfect for my father to jam into his overcoat pocket as he sprinted to the bus each morning.

One thing no one seemed to care for was Tony's '64 Rambler station wagon, modified with dual carbs and glass packs. He'd rev that car up every Sunday morning, fiddling with the choke or resetting the idle. But he only got it out of the driveway once and that was after he was drafted and came back, two years later, with a bushy mustache, a missing rib, and half crazy.

One day, when I was ten, coming home from Little League practice and unwrapping a new package of baseball cards (two doubles, Twins' team picture, Cleon Jones and Bruce Kison), I took a forbidden shortcut through the woods behind the street and came up the Aiellos' driveway.

I bumped into Tony Aiello, who had his mother in an armlock and the sharp end of a spade placed against her throat.

He turned suddenly, forcing Mrs. Aiello around in front of him. Tony was dressed in fatigues, and his face was splotched in gray and green paint. The colors made his eyes look bright.

"I'm waiting for the CO," he said, walking backward up the porch steps, keeping his mother between him and me. Mrs. Aiello's face was hidden in the crook of her son's arm. Then Tony pointed the edge of the spade at me: "Don't try anything," he said.

"I won't, Tony," I said—or croaked, really. "I'm just going home. I bought some baseball cards, and now I'm going home." (I felt this need to explain myself.) I walked away, looking at my cards, acting as if nothing were wrong or different. When I came in the door I was breathing so hard I passed out. I don't remember talking when I came to, but my mother would tell me later I had said something about Tony and the shovel. She ran over to the Aiellos'—in anger, I suppose, at her son's upset— but came back quiet, almost subdued. My mother never talked about it. This story was pieced together.

After the incident with his mother, Tony moved out— or stormed out, blowing out of the garage in his Rambler, skidding away with three fenders, one headlight, and no plates. The neighbors tried to help her, tried to keep her in touch, but soon baseball games were played in November and transparent rain hats could hide pink curlers.

Except for soup stock, we don't see much of Mrs. Aiello anymore. Occasionally, my father helps around her house—he put a new roof on her side porch last year and painted the casement windows. But mostly it's the soup stock, given like forgiveness in a black steamer pot.

My mother slides open the dining-room window. "When do you want to eat?" she asks.

"Did you ask William?" (When I call my father *William* instead of Dad or Bill, it makes her laugh.)

"He said around five."

"Five? Sure. All right."

She closes the dining-room window and locks it—although the street has always been safe. When it comes to protection, my mother is ever-watchful. We have an eight-room house and seven smoke alarms. At eighteen, I have no curfew but come home early anyway; she won't sleep until I'm in. I'm almost used to that.

It's a trait handed down from her mother, this penchant for security. When my grandmother died a few years ago, the lawyers had to break three Yale locks to get to her will. She gave most of her belongings away; no one was surprised. She had already lost much of herself when her first husband died. My mother was the product of a second, loveless marriage. As I pull the leaves from beneath the pine tree, I remember what my mother told me about this mysterious man, whose death at nineteen hung over my grandmother's living. I don't know the actual story, but this is how I imagine it:

In a sailboat (he was a sailor) off Gloucester (she was from Boston), my grandmother leans against the mast. A young woman, she's wearing tennis whites and white canvas shoes that will harden and crust once dry. Dry like his—she looks at his shoes: gray, peeling, the little toe of each foot peering through the small rips around the eyelets. He squints into the evening autumn sun.

"When we head home, we'll run," he says.

He has been promising that all day: "We'll run." My grandmother isn't sure what it means, exactly. Then his voice, loud against the sea gulls and fancy motorboats, raises a notch: "We'll run," he says again, a command now. *"Brace yourself."*

She does. As he eases out the main sail and pulls the tiller to, the boat suddenly leaps, as if yanked from beneath. She has never run.

"To the side," he says, again a command, but he's smiling.

She obeys. They tuck their feet beneath a wooden bar and lean back. She is laughing now, her long brown hair tipping into the broken reflection of the sun on the water. They are moving so fast, her laughter is nearly lost in the surging wake that follows and widens behind them....

I stop raking and watch my father struggling with overloaded trash bags stuffed with leaves from the backyard. He drops the bags on the curb and straightens up, showing off his strict posture—a holdover from the Navy (another sailor). He turns and stares down the driveway, thinking, or trying to remember something.

That's the thing about my father. We talk all the time, we get along fine—but I never know what he's thinking.

I start raking again, moving underneath the hedges, imagining more stories about my grandmother:

Buoys in the Gloucester harbor ring unevenly in the twilight sea. This late in the season, only a few boats remain. From the shore, the masts of the other boats are dark shadows flattened against the horizon. Somewhere—my grandmother can't tell where—a rolled jib pulls against its cleat; the rope moans as it tightens, in symphony with the buoy bells.

"You must be cold—your hair's very wet," he says, using her proffered hand to help himself ashore. "The boat's set; we can clean up and eat. You can dry your hair by the fire."

"There's no fireplace in my hotel room," my grandmother says.

"I know," he says, pulling at the dock knot one last time. "There's one in mine."

She turns, suddenly, from the harbor masts and buoy bells to face him full.

"I'm leaving in two days," he pleads.

While my father places trash bags by my pile of leaves, I think: *I know all the facts of this story. My grandfather went off to war, came back on leave to marry my grandmother on August 11, 1918, and was killed in action in the Argonne Forest on November 4—seven days before the peace was signed. As a result, my grandmother miscarried her child at five months—a boy she named Mark, the name I've been given. But my imagination stops well before this ending: I cannot see my grandmother in bed with a man, much less making love. Yet, of course, it must have happened.*

My father uses wire cutters to prune the small dead twigs on the apple tree in the corner of the yard. "Here," he says, tossing me an apple.

The skin is startling: blood red, and so shiny it looks unreal.

He is standing on a short ladder that sways against the pliant branches of the young tree. I abandon my raking and stand behind him, steadying the ladder with my weight, chewing on the blood-red apple. An early spring has made this harvest rich and full; the season primes my memory as well.

A few weeks ago I uncovered my yearbook from Madison Junior High—our ninth-grade "graduation," three years ago. I was laughing at some of the faces and showed my father a criminal portrait of Rudy Murdoch. We both laughed; my father works with Rudy's dad. Then my father went to the attic and returned with a yearbook from Mount Union College, when he was in the Navy. It was meant for my benefit, but I think he got more out of it. He started calling some of his teachers by their original and vulgar nicknames—whispering some so Mom wouldn't hear. Every pictured cadet seemed to have a story: Joseph "Pig" Pegonni, who used to hide Clark bars in the rafters of the latrine; Wendall Wilson, who regularly spotted mistakes in the chemistry answer book but had failed to bed Linda Levy, "the most generous woman we knew," my father said. And Michael Miller, four-time all-service bantam-weight boxing champ, and Louis Newhouser, and...

Somewhere between the Flahertys and Fuscellos an envelope dropped out of the yearbook. I picked it up—the uneven script was my father's handwriting, addressed to Lt. (jg) Dolph Flynn, USN, stationed at some base in the Philippines. The postage was canceled but another stamp announced, "Return to Sender." Below that were three simple letters: "KIA"—Killed In Action.

My father took the envelope from me and put it back in its place.

"Dolph," he said, as if the name would mean something to me. "A guy I knew in the war, a good guy. There was a distillery near our first Navy base that sold a brand of sour mash called *George Dickle*. It wasn't a big name back then, just a small company. But Dolph knew about it, and used to say, 'One day, Willy, I'm gonna get you Dicklized.' And one day he did. He grew up around here, had a nice big family—ate dinner with them once..."

He closed the yearbook abruptly and said, "You should probably start on that history project you've been talking about all week. Remember that C last semester." Then he disappeared upstairs, back into the attic.

I was glad he had stopped where he did because I didn't want to know anymore. But something bothered me. When he took the letter from me, I noticed it hadn't been opened—by anyone, not even my father. I couldn't imagine it: writing a letter to someone—a friend—and the letter is returned, and not opening it again, not finding out what you had said. And now, forty years later, wouldn't you want to know? To find out what you had written, what had seemed important, what had been preserved here? I stopped imagining, feeling too confused to think about it any longer.

From his perch on the ladder, my father shakes the tree. Suddenly, the air is full of falling apples. I duck and step away from the tree, apples raining around me. My father climbs down from the ladder and examines the fallen fruit, stuffing the good ones into his pockets. I go back to the leaves, filling the large trash bags. I finish the last load just as my mother calls us for dinner.

We're having Mrs. Aiello's soup with steak sandwiches. As my mother puts out the ironstone bowls and handfuls of oyster crackers for us to share, I think about what my friend Lasky will ask me on Monday—the same thing he's been asking me every week since school started: "Did you do it? Did you do it yet?" And I'll tell him no, and he'll tell me to get off my political ass and register for the draft. We'll make plans to visit the post office or see the guidance counselor. "It's easy," Lasky says—but he'll forget by Wednesday and won't mention it again until next week.

As we bow our heads to say grace, I stare at the cloudy broth.

Bless, O Lord, thy gifts to our use...

Fragments of sliced onion and celery float to the surface of the hot, oily soup.

...and us to thy service...

Mrs. Aiello once told my mother that the recipe has been in her family for years, passed down from generation to generation without interruption.

...through Jesus Christ, our Lord...

In the failing light of autumn, I can see my dark reflection staring back at me like a too-familiar photograph in an old family album. I am the picture of my father. I am the picture of my mother. I am the picture of Tony Aiello.

Amen.

STANDING STILL—failing to change—means that your well of rationalization can never run dry. When Jesus said, "It is easier for a camel to pass through an eye of a needle than for a rich man to enter the kingdom of heaven," I'll bet his disciples all had the same thought: either we have to find a very small camel or a very big needle. Our ability to be rational has vaulted us to the top of the evolutionary heap; our ability to rationalize may one day kill us.

Jesus Was a Carpenter

I recently inherited a temporary office with a huge picture window that faces north Oakland.

"The window is great," I said to my boss, "except people in the next building can catch me sleeping."

My boss stared at me. "Don't you recognize that building?"

I looked again and blushed. Our neighbor is the Association for the Blind. Asleep or not, I would forever be invisible to the residents inside.

Sometimes I look across at the red bricks and smoked glass, and wonder what the world looks—well, *feels*—like to the people inside. A world of texture, but not of color. A world of heightened senses and maybe regret. The sight of a blind person fills us sighted folk with a quick wash of emotions: awe, pity, respect, sympathy. Yet one feeling dominates all others—lucky. How outrageously fortunate we are. The lottery wheel spun, and someone else's number came up. For a fleeting moment, as we hurry past the gentleman with the clicking white cane, we wonder when *we're* next for fortune's wheel.

Of course, it's not always just chance. Some actively pursued their handicap with bad decisions, and sometimes we judge them accordingly. Your cousin Shirley's acid trip in college caused her to stare into the sun until her retinas fried. Well, she should've known better. Meanwhile, Shirley dwells on what might have been and dreams that some miracle will let her see just one more sunset.

I've been thinking of *my* cousins recently, those distant cousins in Germany. If my grandparents are any indication, I come from decent, simple stock of middle-class *Volk* who worked the land or worked a machine. If they were political (which, genetically, I doubt), their focus was on the price of bread or the availability of mutton.

My friend Michael had German cousins, too—*had,* past tense. From what he describes, they led similar working-class lives, carefully watching the turning seasons or the turning lathe. Their paths may have crossed somewhere—maybe my cousin Hans borrowed a sickle from Michael's cousin Jacob, and the two commiserated about the skittish weather.

That's what I like to think. What's more likely is that my cousin leaned on his shovel, watching impassively as trainload after trainload of human cargo wound its way through the rolling green countryside on their way to Auschwitz and Belzec. Perhaps, for a fleeting moment, their eyes met—my cousin's and Michael's cousin's— through the cracks in the boxcar. Then the train heaved onward, and Hans returned to his shovel, cursing the random splinters in his palms.

Jesus had splinters—he must have, the carpenter's son. He must have sworn under his breath as some errant sliver found its way into his ring finger as he filed a finish onto a new stool or a chair.

Or a cross.

He started preaching at thirty; that's at least ten or fifteen years as an apprentice in his foster father's shop. The odds are there; he must have fashioned a cross or two. With his gift of vision and history, he must have understood the irony of it all. We can only imagine what he thought, and my imagination tells me he plucked out the splinter and finished the cross on time.

It's a question of ownership; how much is ours? What part of our past do we accept, and what do we dismiss? As a fortunate accident of fortune's wheel, I can't pick and choose my past. Christ built a cross, Michael's relatives called for Barabbas, and my cousins allowed six million of their fellow human beings to disappear without ever asking why. The shower walls of Treblinka are literally crisscrossed with grooves as ten thousand victims tried to claw their way out. One of those gouges is mine; another belongs to you.

Every drop of blood that falls in Tibet or Cambodia or Gallipoli or Iraq lands upon our shoes and splatters the hem of our best suit. Another baby dies in Ethiopia because he didn't get his kwashiorkor shot because I didn't write the check. It's still there, under the stapler in my new office with the big window; and I am safe, because the blind people across the way will never know that I am fast asleep.

(With apologies to Kurt Vonnegut.)

IN THE 1930s, fearful of a German invasion, the French government built a series of trenches and battlements along its border with Germany. History teaches us the futility of such preparations, but war minister Andre Maginot must have missed that class. When the Nazis attacked, the Maginot Line repelled the panzer tanks for the better part of seven minutes. Since then, it's become a famous, deadly symbol of wishful thinking.

Under the weight of such repeated failures, you'd think we would've learned what Robert Frost knew all along—before we build a fence, we should know what we're walling in or walling out.

The Maginot Line

My friend Brian and I made a last-minute trip to a Pat Matheny concert. Outside the ticket window were the usual cadre of scalpers, where we negotiated a price and made our purchase. Just then a young, professionally dressed couple emerged from a Saab asking, "Does someone wish to purchase two extra tickets?"

"I'll give you ten bucks each," our scalper said. "The concert's about to begin."

"No, Frank," said the woman to her husband, who seemed to be a veteran of such "mutual" decision-making. "We paid seventeen-fifty."

The scalper smiled weakly. "Lady, I'm about to head home. Do you want ten bucks for your ticket or not?"

"No, Frank," the woman said. "We paid seventeen-fifty. It's the principle." She marched into the concert, husband in tow, principles held high.

And clearly out twenty bucks.

"Wow," my friend Brian said in a stage whisper, "that's telling 'em!"

When I stopped laughing—perhaps a week later—it occurred to me how often I've seen the scene. God sends us a gift horse, and we spend our energy feeling for its mouth so we can kick it squarely in the teeth.

Give us an inch and we'll bitch. Ask us if the glass is half empty or half full, and we'll say it's *all* empty. How's the weather? Too hot. Too cold. Too humid. Too dry. Too—I don't know—*fickle*. Can't rely on weather these days; it acts too much like, well, weather.

Country music sings it true. Someone strum G7 so I can pine for the girl who got away. If, by chance, she comes back, then I'll sing about the *other* one who got away. Or I'll get drunk and crack up my pickup, then complain when she doesn't throw bail. When she finally tires of this nonsense and leaves for good, then I'll be able to sob with some authority. Please, mister, please—don't play B17—a song like (I'm not making this up) "Your Wife's Been Cheatin' on Us Again."

This isn't a modern phenomenon; our unhappiness dates back centuries. (It may be the winter of our discontent, but we've had a good spring and fall.) The Bible, for instance, is gorged with Gloomy Guses. Rain down some nasty plagues upon Egypt until the Pharaoh finally gives the Jews their freedom, and their first words are, "What took so long?" (Had I been the Pharaoh, everyone could've left after the "festering boils" incident.) Part the Red Sea so they can escape captivity, and their response is, "What? No food? We were better off as slaves!" So send down some manna from heaven—whole wheat, no choles- terol—and that'll make them happy, right? "What good is bread without something to drink?" Okay, so you bring forth water from the ground (a desert, mind you) and they'll finally show their appreciation—by building a golden calf. Talk about insults! Sort of makes Billy Martin look like Miss Manners, doesn't it?

Why are we so dissatisfied? Why is nothing ever enough? What is *wrong* with us, anyhow?

Here's my guess: we don't know how to be loved.

Deep down, down past the sighing, the sulking, the endless complaints, we cannot accept who we are or what we've been given. What looks like ingratitude may well be insecurity *(I cannot believe you love me, so I'll complain about how you show it)* or fear *(This operation scares the hell out of me, but I'll bad-mouth the hospital food instead)* or confusion *(I've forgotten why we're fight- ing, but I can't tell you how much I need you or how sorry I am, so I'll just wait until we get tired enough to make up).*

And because we cannot accept ourselves, anyone who offers unconditional love—let's say God, for the sake of argument—is automatically the target of our irrational wrath. "If only my wife hadn't been so damned good," says the drunkard Hickey in O'Neill's *The Iceman Cometh.* "But it was written all over her face, sweetness and love and pity and forgiveness...so I killed her."

It infuriates us: God as Mister Rogers, accepting us at face value, just for who we are—scalpers, drunkards, country-music singers—when, in fact, we cannot accept ourselves. It's as if we've built an emotional Maginot Line, if we're constantly suspicious of acceptance, then no amount of rejection will surprise us. Yet, time and again, despite our careful defenses, rejection *does* surprise us. So we vow, "Never again! Never again! If anyone's going to shoot me in the foot, why I'll beat 'em to it!"

"Wow," my friend Brian would say, "that's telling 'em!"

You would think that by now we would have worn ourselves out with pouting. But our cache of misery seems limitless. Maybe one day we'll grow weary of whining and celebrate the rain, the manna, the half-filled glass of water, the little gifts from heaven that make each day bearable. Instead of cloaking ourselves in the armor of pessimism, maybe we'll concede that we are who we are: capricious, unfortunate, wonderful, delicate, alive. Forgiven.

YOU, NEIGHBOR GOD, if sometimes in the night
I rouse you with loud knocking, I do so
only because I seldom hear you breathe
and know: you are alone.
And should you need a drink, no one is there
to reach it to you, groping in the dark.
Always I harken. Give but a small sign.
I am quite near.

         –RAINER MARIA RILKE

Elvis, Bok Choy,
and Belief

I had this dream: I was in Shop 'n Save pushing a cart with two babies (neither of them mine) and four watermelons (all mine, I suppose). I was looking for a cereal called Animal Crackers Spaghetti because I had a coupon for seven dollars off.

In the condiments aisle, I saw Elvis.

It was the Elvis of 1971—the bell-bottoms, the side-burns, the open-necked shirt and fly-me lapels, but before he needed the prize belt for his stomach. He was hefting two jars of pickled herring, apparently weighing the difference in price. Finally, he gave that Elvis shrug and put one of the jars away. Then he looked at me and seemed embarrassed that I had caught him.

"This one's low salt," he drawled, holding up one jar of herring. Then, spying my two new children, he gave me that smile/snarl that used to slay 'em in Vegas. "You're a very lucky man," Elvis said to me, then turned and walked away, bell-bottoms swinging, toward the bok choy in the produce section.

My reaction in my dream was the same as if I had been awake: *Maybe he is alive,* I thought.

The real Shop 'n Save doesn't stock Animal Crackers Spaghetti, but it does carry all of the tabloids: "I Had Bigfoot's Baby" or "Aliens Fixed My Transmission" or "Liberace Buried in Lenin's Tomb." Every week, somewhere between the horoscope and "They'll Do It Every Time" cartoon is yet another Elvis sighting. ("Mrs. Alice D. Whitless of Poduck, Montana, claims legendary rock star Elvis Presley cured her son's prickly heat with an ordinary flashlight and a teaspoon of Crisco.") And even though you laugh at the headlines as you stand in the checkout line, in the back of your mind you're thinking, *Maybe he is alive. Could all those people be lying?*

In a recent poll, one out of ten Americans surveyed believe that Elvis Presley isn't really dead. We now have more Elvis believers than we do Episcopalians. What is God trying to tell us?

My college friends are relentlessly cynical. (Our collective adolescence coincided with Watergate, which explains a lot.) They seem puzzled by my faith, suspicious that I could, well, *sell out* to religion. (Actually, the subject doesn't come up much; we respect each other's belief—and besides, Pitt's ahead by seven at the half...) They'll never say it, but beneath their knotted brow is the obvious question, "What happened to *you?*"

I can't answer. I didn't have a conversion experience (except about Astroturf), I'm not born again, and I remain a sinner of extraordinary weakness. My attendance at church must amuse my friends. I haven't matured a whit since college. I still fight raging hormones and raging insecurities, still swear at my feckless luck with cars and money. When Saint Peter asks for an account of my life at the Pearly Gates, I will tell him, "I spent my life looking for store receipts and jumper cables."

So why bother with church?

Humilitas veritas est, Pliny the Younger said—"Humility is truth." Okay, Pliny was a pagan, but it still hits home. When I walk into Assumption Church in Bellevue or Calvary in Shadyside, I am both burdened and free. I squirm under the weight of my trespasses—things done and left undone—and feel liberated by the undeserved love of another: the gifts of God for the people of God. At the consecration, while others bow their heads, I raise mine; I want to witness the sight of my roommates on this planet, all of them *on their knees.* During the week their lusts rage, their cars won't start, their checkbooks won't balance, their prejudices run amok; but for this singular moment, they are humble in spite of themselves. Together, we foolishly resolve to mend our ways starting first thing tomorrow—knowing tomorrow will begin like any other Monday, with one finger out the window on the Parkway.

Why bother? Why *not* bother? Why not acknowledge our infantile frailty in the face of history and ask for help and guidance? Why not bow our heads in forgiveness for our role in the human tragedy? Why not bend our knees in a prayer for humility: "Lord, I am not worthy to receive you, but only say the word and I shall be healed"?

"But what about *doubt?*" my friends would ask.

Doubt sits next to me in the pew. He reads the bulletin during the sermon with his feet propped up on the kneeler. He picks his teeth with a torn corner of the hymnal. Sometimes he snores. But every Sunday at the sign of peace, I turn and shake Doubt's hand. His grip almost breaks my knuckles. I envy those who are seated far away from Doubt, but I choose to come back each week, knowing Doubt will find me wherever I sit.

Which reminds me of my brother. Kevin is a walking treasure of TV trivia. (He knows *both* versions of the *Gilligan's Island* theme.) His favorite show is/was *Star Trek,* but there's always a catch. Midway through every episode, Kirk orders Sulu to "fire phasers," and one is treated to the sound of phasers firing in space.

"There's no sound in space!" Kevin screams at the set. "It's a basic law of physics!"

Kevin can accept Mr. Spock, who's half-human, half-Vulcan; he can accept folks on other planets speaking

English; he can even accept Lieutenant Uhura wearing miniskirts in the twenty-second century—but *sound in space?!* There are *limits* to credibility...

And that, I suppose, explains my faith. Each week is a test of my own credibility; do I come here for solace only, and not for strength? For pardon only, and not for renewal? Am I blinded by the liturgy, content to turn my spiritual life over to tradition rather than seek my own expression? Or is it exactly in those centuries of believers who follow the ageless words of prayer that I find my own small place in the world?

I wish my faith were certain. Instead, I take comfort where I find it and wrestle demons when I must. Despite the endless sightings and screaming headlines, I choose to believe the truth as I know it: Elvis is dead, and—by the grace of God—life goes on.

BACK IN THE HALYCON DAYS before I could drive—
back before my garage became a hospice for automobiles—we grade school guys used to dream about our
Dream Cars. Most of my classmates drooled over pic-
tures of Corvettes and Barracudas and Javelins. Me? I
longed for a Corvair—a red one with white-walls, maybe
a convertible. Of course, it was later learned that driving
a Corvair was about as safe as being a fly at a frog
festival. I should have known then....I should have
known that cars would be my albatross, and that I was
destined to repeat this same sad story the rest of my
days.

A Wing and a Prayer

My relationship with cars has been nothing short of
tragic. I have become the Simon of Cyrene to
automobiles, helping them limp along to their
sorrowful appointment with destiny.

Part of the problem, I admit, is me. I buy needy cars the
way some people gravitate toward needy lovers. While
my wife seems inexplicably enamored with Solid & Reli-
able (Attorneys-at-Law), I take on the welfare cases,
convinced that a little oil and a lot of TLC will magically
correct a recalcitrant transmission that will only go from
second to third when the moon is in the seventh house.

Besides, I've always been partial to late bloomers. (I

myself expect to bloom any decade now. Some people are born to greatness; some earn it. I'm patiently waiting for greatness to be thrust upon me.) So there I am, asking why a six-year-old Honda costs only $1,850. The seller paws the dirt with his shoe and mutters sheepishly, "It's got some miles."

"Like how many?" I ask, hoping for the best.

"A little over a hundred thousand," he says. "Or a lot—a hundred fifty thousand. Maybe one eighty...I haven't checked recently."

"That's *great!*" I say, and gleefully write the check, convinced once again that I've made the deal of the century. Of course, my cheerful mood breaks the same moment the timing belt breaks, and my mechanic shakes his head as I rail against the so-and-so who would sell me this piece of junk. My mechanic says nothing. He can't; I'm putting his daughter through school. I became suspicious when her tuition bills came addressed to me.

But part of the blame lies squarely with fate. I own a Japanese jeep, which, like an old dog, knows but one trick: rolling over. I finally tired of paying insurance premiums that rivaled the Peruvian national debt, so a used car lot in Washington, Pennsylvania, agreed to sell it for me—for a price. And a few months later, some discerning young man drove my jeep off the lot. Well, not "off the lot" as much as *though the gate*, which was locked because technically the lot wasn't open, because—strictly speaking—he was stealing my car.

After a short test drive, the young man decided against the jeep, so he parked into the back of another car for safekeeping. A week later, my car was returned to me—

well, most of it; the fender and a few tie rods stayed behind in Washington, Pennsylvania. Eight hundred fifty dollars later, why it looked practically new. Of course, my insurance rates went up, a standard surcharge anytime an accident occurs, especially during the commission of a felony.

In keeping with my suicidal outlook, I still have the jeep. Recently, I returned to it late one evening to find the side window smashed. As best I can figure it, the person wanted to steal either the car or my cassette tapes, but once inside decided against both. I felt a little hurt, frankly. I can't imagine why a pirated Tony Bennett tape wouldn't be appealing.

Why labor you with my troubles? Because I think there's a lesson here (in addition to several obvious morals about high miles and needy cars). We want from our cars what we need but can't get from life, like great mileage, responsiveness, brakes, and seat belts. We want a life that's full throttle on the open road, yet one we can still steer calmly through the chaos of city streets. We want a life that pops open an air bag when we're about to go headlong into another disastrous endeavor. We want a life insurance policy that will pay for our bad decisions—and no deductible. We want to feel the road when the curves get exciting, but we want to feel nothing when the going gets bumpy. And—more than anything—we want cruise control.

We want what we cannot have.

Instead, our lives run like a '74 Volkswagen. The steering is spotty, and one unmoored headlight nods up and down at oncoming traffic. There's no air bag, and the brakes are so shoddy they piddle fluid all over the drive-way.

You complain bitterly, but every morning that old heap starts. And you think, as the VW winds its way through the gears, that maybe it's grace from heaven above that pushes you onto life's highway for yet another run on the two-lane blacktop. It's a piece of junk, but it's *your* piece of junk. And you've kept it going all these years on the same two jimmied ingredients: a wing and a prayer.

Well, God bless you both.

STORY HAS IT THAT GOD MADE EVE from Adam's rib—and Adam's sons have spent the balance of history chasing Eve's daughters, trying to reconnect with that lost piece of themselves.

It's lust, pure and simple. We decry lust as evil, but it's the same healthy impulse that keeps the species going. In true paradoxical fashion, we're given the innate desire to be with that One Special Someone fully and completely—and a nearly equal desire to sabotage that relationship with a wandering eye. As we stumble from adolescence (when we're Hormones with Legs) into adulthood, we face the most challenging change of all: learning *not* to change partners at a moment's notice, but to discover the many sides of that One Special Someone who shares our journey with us, who understands our weaknesses, and who knows when to kick us really hard in the half-moons of flab just beneath our lower cheeks.

Of course, such challenges are not without trial...

Angel

Okay, it was late, and the bachelor party had left us too well-oiled, so when someone suggested The Cricket—a local topless bar—it seemed to make perfect sense.

There's a bar in the front of the building; in the back is

the runway, with gaudy curtains, loud music, and real bad lighting. Every twenty minutes or so, another young woman with a name like Bambi or Angel or Brandi struts out on stage dressed in very little, and—by the end of her three-song "act"—she's wearing even less.

The front seats are crowded with a cadre of equally well-oiled white males, anxiously offering folded dollar bills to Bambi or Angel or Brandi. The back rows are reserved for the veterans—men who come here every night or every other night, just to stare, just to jump-start a little excitement in their monstrously mundane lives.

Bambi and Angel and Brandi couldn't care less. Although they have all the practiced techniques—the high heels, the gyrations, the teasing looks—they are, in fact, bordering on bored. For them, it truly is an *act,* one they neither enjoy nor detest, just another job. If it paid as well, they'd just as likely be asking, "Do you want fries with that?"

As the fog rolls through my head on little Budweiser feet, I survey the clientele. Every eye averts mine, of course—no one wants to be seen here. A huge sign above the runway proclaims, "No contact with the dancer's (sic) permitted," but it could just as easily read, "No human contact of any kind permitted." Despite the wolf whistles, the noise, the imitations of intimacy, I decide that this is the loneliest place in America.

And here I sit.

In the back of my mind, I can still hear Sister Alenita's words: "Sin is an offense to God." She broke it down further into mortal and venial sins, but decades of active repression have washed away the distinction. Later, at

Central Catholic, Brother Richard (whom we all thought was "cool," even though he was a Brother), defined sin as the absence of God.

Funny...despite the years of religious rote drilled into my brain, I didn't feel like a sinner at The Cricket—at least not in Sister Alenita's terms. But Brother Richard was right: God was long gone from here, not even leaving a half-filled beer behind. We were all alone—Bambi and Angel, the white guys and me, a confederacy of strangers, swilling like hogs from the testosterone well.

Do I sound like a Puritan? Do I sound like Jerry Falwell's Catholic cousin? Don't get me wrong—I didn't avert my eyes when Angel came on stage. But after it was over, it seemed like something had been taken from me, that I had given Angel my crumpled dollar, and all I was left with was a black hole just above my left ventricle, where part of myself leaked out into the void.

It's not about sex. It's not about nudity, the obvious chauvinism, the money changing hands. It's about the bad lighting—it's the sin of pretense, of mistaking skin for flesh, of substituting the security of the stripper for the capriciousness of real relationships. As much as we press against the cheesy footlights waving our dollars, working our way as close as the bouncer will allow, we're really pulling away, sounding retreat from the uncertainty of actual intimacy. Instead, we'll opt for imitation; we'll side on the side of illusion, safe from rejection, safe from the difficult work of bridge building, protected from the deathlike threat of vulnerability.

But, as with most shortcuts, there's a price to pay. By choosing the runway, we delay once again our journey toward each other. Despite the celebratory mood—the drinks, the hoots, Bambi's sparkling G-string—we're really recoiling into ourselves, refining our fantasies instead of our friendships. When the evening ends, we well-oiled white males will trip out into the cool air, our eyesight dimmed by hours of poor lighting, straining to see in the real darkness of the night. Tomorrow will greet us with a pounding headache and blinding sunlight, the folded bills disappeared from our pockets.

In my imagination I see Angel fast asleep. On her nightstand is a stack of ones; Angel is saving for a better life.

As I wait for the aspirin to take effect, I wonder: if only I had saved my dollars like Angel, maybe I wouldn't feel so empty right now.

Maybe I need to take better care of my investments.

IN AUGUST OF 1989, Dave Drevecky, star pitcher of the San Francisco Giants, came back from cancer surgery to pitch a four-hitter against the Cincinnati Reds. Baseball writers exhausted their on-line thesauruses looking for superlatives. "Courageous" came in first, followed by "heroic" and "greatest comeback of all time."

I have never met Dave Drevecky. He seems like a nice guy, and I'm glad he's feeling better. But "courageous comeback"? He left as a pitcher, and he came back as—um—a pitcher. That's his job, and what he loves to do. If he came back as an accountant, now *that* would be something. Or an ironworker. Or if an ironworker came back from chemotherapy to be a major-league pitcher....

But we're unable to deal with such complex alternatives. We need simple stories with straightforward heroes. We need our legends, with no complications. We need storybook endings.

Such endings are swell for storybooks and baseball, but we know better about everything else. If the changes in our lives are to have any redemptive power, we've got to accept the whole weird novel, not just our favorite chapters. And that means accepting some strange plot twists and really quirky character traits.

Myth Take

It is typical of myth that cruel facts are welded together with beneficent ones...how healing is such a myth *to the person who can find and live with it!* (Rollo May)

Albert Einstein never flunked math. Never came close. Actually, he was never a bad student; occasionally he disrupted class, but that was about it.

He did work in the Swiss Patent Office, but not as a last resort. Many of the patent applications involved difficult technical processes. He was hired because he was *smart*, not because he couldn't find other work. His skill and his talent were recognized eventually, if not immediately. Like many people, it took more than one attempt to get his dissertation completed. He was considered competent as an instructor; he was never considered "a failure."

He was very, very good in math. He was not a world-class mathematician, but he knew enough to work out enormously complicated proofs. There's some question about how much he "borrowed" from other physicists; there's also a question of how much other physicists tried to attribute his findings to themselves.

No record shows that he was more forgetful than you or I—or less forgetful. He was as concerned about money as you and I.

Like many of us, Einstein's public persona was different from his private persona. Publicly, he was ethical and moral and kind. Privately, one can only guess, but some evidence suggests he chased women. His first child was fathered out of wedlock. He was occasionally an indifferent parent and husband; other times, he was generous.

In other words, he was as ordinary and as exceptional as the rest of us. Except that he changed the face of physics forever.

That's not the Einstein you know, is it? The wild-haired, head-in-the-clouds, absent-minded pacifist professor—that's more like it, eh? But we've created a myth, and now we can't extract ourselves from it.

Why do we want Einstein to be someone else? After all, isn't revolutionizing our concept of the universe enough? Why do we have to make him more—or less—than who he really was?

The short answer is easy: we want purity. We want a saint so we canonize those whose accomplishments seem other-worldly: athletes whose outrageous agility stuns us earthbound spectators; politicians like Lincoln and Washington, who transformed our nation; or the "physically challenged" folks who, like physicist Stephen Hawking, "overcame personal tragedy" to "triumph" in their chosen fields. (Instead of "physicist Stephen Hawking," it's always "quadriplegic Stephen Hawking." Never mind his native talent, focus on the wheelchair. Just give us a label and we'll be happy.)

Well, Stephen Hawking has left his wife, and who knows why? Apparently, he's *not* eternally grateful for the support she's given him through two decades of marriage and disease. Instead, he's one of us: complicated, inconsistent, gifted, and surprising.

Complexity confuses us. When my friend Sally was pulled over by the police for doing fifty in a thirty-five-mile-per-hour zone, she was sure they were mistaken. "I'm not the kind of person who gets tickets," she said, as if she were immune. It's the logic of shock: despite the overwhelming evidence, we still rewrite history to fit our reality. If the proof doesn't fit our package, we'll get ourselves a new package. And so our myths are preserved: Thomas Jefferson never owned slaves, Lincoln wrote the Gettysburg Address on the back of an envelope in one draft, Joe DiMaggio never struck out, Uncle Harry is not an alcoholic. There. We're safe.

But safe from what? We know better. We know that life doesn't come in neat boxes, but we insist on fantasy. That's why gossip abounds. We tsk-tsk at each failing of Britain's royal family or cluck over the latest Hollywood star to check into drug rehab. *Their* inconsistencies are *our* wonderment—as if our own families aren't just as screwed up.

Jesus was a lot of things, but consistent wasn't one of them. Maybe the gospels disagree because they had different authors—or maybe Jesus said different things on different days. It fits with the label "true God and true man," the ultimate paradox. And it fits with the times: Jerusalem in chaos, a city under foreign occupation. Even when he left this world, his followers offered truly differing accounts of his work. Saint Paul provides amazingly inconsistent instructions, often within the same epistle.

Yet the central message of Christ has survived for two thousand years. It's a message of hope and forgiveness and acceptance. It's mixed with anger and impatience and a challenge to authority. Turn the other cheek, Jesus says, then he turns over the moneychangers' tables. Perhaps the divine message survives because the messenger is so human.

Our myths about Christ cannot survive scrutiny. We're forced to confront who we are and who we're capable of becoming. We're left with a model of our own weakness and our own strengths but also of one who tried to change the world he saw and died for his convictions. And we're confronted with the power of what we know to be true, stripped of myths and inconsistencies: your neighbor is yourself, and if we're to suffer through the millenia, we'd better act accordingly.

Meanwhile, we'll stagger forward each day, living by our wits and our myths. We're the final proof that Einstein was right. He discovered the ironclad law of objects in motion, objects like us. *Everything is relative.* Life is a mysterious puzzle. The universe is like a child's car seat with the fake steering wheel. We try to navigate the turns and we beep our little plastic horns, but it's all a myth. Someone else is driving, and the best we can do is strap ourselves in and enjoy the ride.

—*With thanks to John Norton*

WHILE DOING RESEARCH for an article on alcoholism, I began attending recovery meetings. Though I am not an alcoholic, those meetings changed my life. Amidst the pain, the regrets, the loneliness—and the hope—my faith emerged with more clarity than ever before. On my darkest days, I still attend meetings and feel once again the power of those twelve simple precepts.

But I found, as many have before me, that faith and conviction aren't enough. "Never trust a zealot," my friend Mike once told me, and it's absolutely true. Faith isn't "found" in platitudes, it's practiced—and sometimes that means tolerating (even encouraging) the doubt that often accompanies discovery and change.

God, Twelve Steps, and the Freshman Comp Teacher

I used to joke with my composition students about their music. "Back in *my* era," I'd say, sounding more like fifty-one than thirty-one, "we had *real* music—none of this 'New Kids' stuff." But they would laugh at "my era," knowing that I teethed on songs like "Disco Duck" and "The Night Chicago Died."

But I don't joke anymore. Something has happened.

All the heroes and legends I knew as a child
Have fallen to idols of clay
I feel this empty place inside
So afraid I've lost my faith...
                              –Styx

While the thirtysomething set listens to cheery, hopeful songs like "From a Distance," the Nintendo generation—now past adolescence—is getting an entirely different message on MTV, more brooding, more uncertain—more adult.

I see the homeless sleeping on a cold dark street
Like bodies in an open grave
Underneath a broken neon sign
That used to read, "Jesus Saves..."
                              –Poison

And their compositions reflect this sense of searching and alienation. "The more I think about my generation, the more I am filled with contempt," one student wrote last term. "They are like cows...." It's a language of isolation and resignation that seems more appropriate to middle age than midterms.

Don't get me wrong; searching is healthy. It's my duty as a teacher to challenge their everyday assumptions and provincial preconceptions. If my students never question their outlook, then I've failed as a teacher.

But that kind of questioning isn't what I'm talking about.

I'm talking about God.

As they say in Twelve Step recovery meetings, I mean "God" however you may imagine God to be—some force in the world that is greater than ourselves. And by that definition, we play God in the classroom—a force greater than our students. It's unique to teachers. We encourage students to open up their lives for examination. (They don't have this conflict at IBM.)

I'd argue even further: we see our mission in moral terms, whether we acknowledge it or not. It's been decided that simplistic thought, stereotypical thought, or easy, baseless judgments have no place in the classroom. But, like it or not, they've certainly found a place *outside* the classroom. There are millions of folks—successful, productive folks—who see no moral dilemma in the plight of the Third World; who don't give a damn about global warming; who don't see racial stereotypes as bad; who feel comfortable in repressive, sexist roles; and who send their children to college, into my classroom. Against that background, my analysis of and response to this eighteen-year-old's essay surely has a moral component.

Consider this: once I think of my students as "victims" of popular culture—television, Rambo, rock music—then I place *my* culture (high culture, academic culture, counterculture) on the moral high ground. To think that college instructors are less prejudiced than other professionals is naive; my biases are subtle and often acceptable, but they are no better.

Ironically, some of my students' favorite rock stars are veterans of the Betty Ford Clinic, where they learned all about recovery and Twelve Steps and staying clean. But I worry that my classroom offers the worst kind of group therapy—perhaps six or seven of the Twelve Steps, just enough to make them question themselves but not enough to help them "get better."

On one hand, I hold absolute power over their grades; on the other, I prompt them to take a fearless self-inventory of their beliefs—all while I "correct" their short-comings, everything from comma splices to their most fundamental convictions. And most students are willing to follow the program to a certain healthy point—until these lessons of critique and examination are no longer constructive. With these students—the majority—we do our job.

But every term there are one or two students who trust the teacher completely and trust their own newly discovered Credo of Reason: *Inquiry Will Lead to Truth.* ("Be fearless and thorough from the very start," Bill W. says. "Some of us have tried to hold on to our old ideas and the result was nil until we let go absolutely.") What of these students, whose only crime was believing in the academic method?

Money doesn't mean much
when you have a razor against your wrist.
                              –student essay

How should I respond to an essay like this? Of course, the easy way out is to go strictly "by the text": note the student's strategies, locate a "voice," analyze the cultural influences—all of which distances me from the student. After all, I've "empowered" these students to share equal-ly in the text and decide their own stance. Then again, the idea of "empowerment" and "shared experience" must seem pretty funny to them when they get their grades.

Instead, inquiry has led to an epiphany of my own. I realize now that I have a single creed in the classroom: avoid simplicity. Strike it down at every turn. Go for the rich. Encourage the complex. It's like a mantra. If I succeed in getting my students to see every angle, to be suspicious of every answer, then I am a "good teacher." I play God whether I like it or not, whether I'm up to the task or not.

But isn't complexity a dangerous goal? Sure, most students will know the limits; they'll understand that revising their beliefs doesn't necessarily mean rejecting their beliefs. But some may not. Some students may continue to do exactly as I have taught them: to question every assumption, every word of every text, every belief, even the teacher, even themselves. I can cover myself by explaining the difference between skepticism and cynicism, but are they still listening? Or has the damage been done?

Despite the similarities to recovery meetings—the same room, the same hour, the same people every week—we leave out the most important of the Twelve Steps: acknowledging a power greater than ourselves. Oh, we talk about the power of words, maybe sometimes about the power of the proletariat; but we hardly ever mention God, let alone "God as you understand him—or her." And that's the way it should be. This ain't Billy Graham.

But if we don't tolerate conversion of the sinful, I wonder if we should tolerate a *loss* of faith. I don't mean faith in the Almighty, I mean faith in *anything*. Does all this constant scrutiny have a goal? Or is it complexity for complexity's sake, as if complexity will keep us warm at night, as if we can wrap our students in books and send them out into the world, content that we have done our job?

Those of you who teach for a living realize that my argument is full of holes. And I don't care. My point is simple, not complex (and that doesn't make it any less valid): as a teacher, you are an influence on your students, an influence that goes beyond margin notes and comma splices. Some students—maybe only one or two a term, but does it matter?—will look to you in the dark hours of their doubt, a doubt you may have helped to refine.

It puts you in a difficult, undesirable position, but it's a fact, and an enormous responsibility. And I want you to think about that. If you don't have an answer, that's okay—just think about it. It's an unfair duty, a wonderful opportunity, just like the rest of life.

And I'll say to you what I said to the student I quoted above—the one about the razor at the wrist. Don't judge a whole lot by one term. You'll change. You may even come to accept yourself for who you are: wonderful, inconsistent, unique, uncertain—much like the rest of humanity. Looking back, I may have been too pat, but that's part of teaching—and learning—for both of us.

I'm fully aware that this is a diatribe offering few options. But instead of concluding with another depressing rock lyric, I'll end with the prayer that's often said at recovery meetings:

> God grant me the serenity to accept the things I cannot change, courage to change the things I can, and the wisdom to know the difference.

MY WIFE SANDEE HAS A THEORY: if social scientists would only ask the right questions, they would find that the leading cause of divorce isn't infidelity or money but not putting the cap back on the toothpaste. Or how one's spouse acts behind the wheel. Or not putting the toilet seat down. It's how we live day to day—and not our suspicions about sex or finances—that truly gauge if marriage is bliss or bust.

Needless to say, one can say the same about going to church once a week versus living our lives from Monday through Friday. It was needless to say, but I said it anyway because as much as I preach about change, I seem to need constant reminders...

Blue Laws and Red Supras

Remember blue laws?

I don't. For as long as I've been in full consciousness, suburban malls have had Sunday hours. Since

I began drinking legally (okay, even before that), there've been Sunday beer sales at the Original Hot Dog Shop on Forbes Avenue so no one would go thirsty while watching the Steelers. And when my mother ran out of salt at five minutes to Sunday dinner, she sent me to the corner grocery, which was (and is) open on Sundays. All day.

Now that my job and marriage have forced me to act like an adult, I'd like to bring back blue laws—no Sunday extras, no malls, no movies, nada.

The goal? No driving on Sundays.

Believe me, it's for everyone's own good, because something about the Sabbath makes motorists crazy. Oh, drivers aren't any better or worse on Sundays—and that's what's disturbing. If you don't have to be at work in five minutes, why did you just blow through that light? Surely you don't drive like that all the time....

One recent Sunday, my wife and I were driving down Penn Avenue on our way to Calvary Church in Shadyside. As I turned from Penn to Fifth, a lovely young woman in a red foreign sports car (a brand-new Toyota Supra GS, but who's counting?) cut me off at the pass. I beeped—more a chauvinistic hiccup than defensive driving—and she responded with a salute of her own. Though she held up only one finger, I'm quite sure she meant two words.

Being the mature, self-actualized individual that I am, I slammed on the gas and the chase was on. But it wasn't exactly a chase; my Chevette has all the pickup speed of an organ donor. The last I saw of her, she was disappearing into the University of Pittsburgh's Oakland campus.

Her license plate read "DRP•DED."

After muttering "gosh darn" or something similar, I

turned back toward the church. Though I was too angry to see the irony, it wasn't lost on my wife.

"I love to see you so caught up in the Christian spirit," she said.

"What's that supposed to mean?" I responded, showing my skill at witty comebacks. My wife gave me the kind of look that made me dread the rest of the day.

So the daring young woman in her flying machine had done more than simply cut me off. She had managed to get my goat, which in turn angered my wife, and (of course) made us late for church. We got there in time for the sermon—something about forgiveness, but I didn't pay much attention. I kept daydreaming about finding DRP•DED parked in Oakland, where I could flatten her tires or stick a potato in her exhaust. My imagination, feverish with revenge, conjured up rich images of retribution. Hell hath no fury like a motorist wronged.

But as we left church, something happened.

An enormous flock of birds alighted on the roof of Sacred Heart Church across the street. Despite the cold weather (or perhaps because of it), the birds began chirping and cawing in unison, creating an unbelievable noise. I stood on the steps of Calvary, watching and listening. Suddenly, Sacred Heart's bells began to toll, calling the faithful to noon services. The startled birds, reacting as a single, connected unit, fled the rooftop. They rose together and descended toward Walnut Street in a frenzied yet unmistakable pattern. The sky was filled with countless birds, beating their wings furiously in beautiful, chaotic, perfect formation, accompanied by the music of church bells.

In that moment, I saw forces at work, forces driven not by ego or revenge or anger, but by something else. I wasn't sure if my wife was watching, but I reached over and squeezed her hand, offering an apology. She hesitated, then squeezed back, though God knows I didn't deserve her forgiveness.

When we reached the car, I noticed that one of the birds—apparently overdosed on berries—had left a small present on my windshield. Nature, that final arbiter of irony, had given me my just reward for acting like a jerk.

As we drove home, I thought: *maybe blue laws aren't such a nuisance after all. Maybe we should be forced to slow our lives down once a week. Without knowing what rest feels like, what pleasure can we get from work?*

But my pastoral thoughts soon faded, and I found myself daydreaming about a huge bird, the size of the *Concorde,* searching the streets of Oakland for a certain red Supra onto which it could unload its precious cargo of revenge.

CHANGE, especially fundamental change, produces heroes of all kinds. We read about famous ones who, caught in the headlights of oncoming history, navigate a greater course for themselves and others. This need for heroic contests is so much a part of our mythic genes that we invent them when we run low. With a perfectly straight face, we'll use language like "titanic battle" and "tragic defeat" to describe a football game—and not necessarily a playoff game.

It proves that Andy Warhol was *almost* correct, because *almost* everyone is famous for fifteen minutes. It's the "almost" that's tricky. With so many changing faces on our pop-culture Mount Rushmore, we don't recognize the everyday heroes who sit next to us on the bus, patiently waging their own epic struggle with life.

Good and Evil (Knievel)

I've been invited to go bungee jumping—that ridiculous fad where grown men and women leap off of bridges in a free-fall, only to be snapped back to safety with an oversized rubber band. "Are you brave enough?" one promotion asks.

No, I guess not.

It's not that I'm a coward (well, that's not the *only*

reason). Nor, as my closet will attest, am I against fads. But I resent the idea of "bravery" here, bravery in the face of insane physical risk.

Pointlessly risking one's neck has always seemed ludicrous. I went to the circus just once; the tightrope walkers scared the hell out of me, so I never went back. Why do they do it? What's the thrill for the audience? What's the attraction of a stare-down contest with death? Evil Knievel made himself famous with such stunts—leaping over cars, over canyons. Karl Wallenda became equally famous for dying the way he lived, firmly gripping the balance pole all the way down.

What's the point?

Of course, one could say the same of Lewis and Clark or Peary and the North Pole or any bunch of space-walking astronauts. "Because it's there," said Edmund Hillary about climbing Mount Everest.

I could have said *"conquered* Mount Everest," but he didn't conquer it. Everest is still there, with a couple dozen flags stuck in its peak. Hillary is too old to climb. Evil Knievel is too old to jump cars. And Karl Wallenda is still dead.

What is "conquered" is fear, the fear of giving in to our own weakness (or common sense). Don't get me wrong—conquering one's fears is a real accomplishment. But let's be sure what it is we're conquering; we've met the enemy, and he (or she) is us.

Now *here's* a story of risk and adventure. Twice each week, Henry T. leaves his house in Bellevue, Pennsylvania, takes two buses (about a ninety-minute ride) to see his wife at the Kane Nursing Home in the South Hills of

Pittsburgh. His wife has Alzheimer's. Despite fifty-two years of marriage, she doesn't know Henry from Adam. He's just another nice face in the room, as fantastic as the nonstop TV images that dart across her weakened eyes.

But this nice face washes her twice a week, making sure to run a towel between her toes so she won't chafe. He turns her, as best as his seventy-eight-year-old body will allow, to dab some A&D ointment on a stubborn bedsore. He combs her hair and always compliments her long white locks—the same locks that first attracted him fifty-two years ago. (She doesn't remember their court-ship or how fine he looked in his uniform.) Nonetheless, he talks to her about their life together, catches her up on baseball and the neighbors, tells her the news of their two grown sons, both of whom live far away.

To her, these stories of youth and marriage and chil-dren are dreamy and senseless. Sometimes she cries for no reason, and he holds her. Sometimes she lashes out at him, calling him "mean, mean," one of the few recogniz-able words she has left (the others are "dove" and "let-ter"). On those days—"Annie had one of her moods," Henry says—the bus trip home is long and sad. But he'll be back on Thursday, smiling as if nothing happened. Sometimes she smiles back. Henry lives for those mo-ments. "That's my Annie," he says.

Father John Gallagher of Assumption Church tells this story, so Henry is famous in Bellevue, Pennsylvania. No one else has heard of him. He doesn't jump over cars, doesn't walk the tightrope, hasn't discovered any poles that we know of.

But think of the risks!

Twice a week, Henry risks his life. He risks everything that's ever meant anything to him: the corporate memory of their five decades together; his children's inheritance, whittled away by private nurses and copayments; his sense of himself as Annie's husband, when really he's become Annie's parent. At his daily Masses, Henry prays for Annie, not for himself. Someone else might pray for Annie's merciful death, but the thought has never crossed Henry's mind because Henry isn't daring death. He's daring life. He's living on the edge, where every visit to Annie means surviving a thousand deaths. For half a century, the team of Henry and Annie leapt over canyons, danced on the high wire, and now run headlong into the Alzheimer's wall—no helmet, no seat belt, no safety net. Death lost its bite long ago.

Well, nothing will make Henry famous. You'll finish reading this, finish your cup of coffee, and Henry's story will be lost in the heap of images that embrace us each day. No matter. Next Thursday, Henry will once again board the 16C Bellevue, the first leg on the adventure of a lifetime.

A STUDENT OF MINE from Russia had the damnedest time translating my oldest daughter's name. "You call her 'Faith'?" he asked, again and again. "This does not make any sense." Finally, it dawned on me. Literally translated, the word means "belief." ("This is my daughter, Belief Collins.") It was as if I named her some arbitrary, awkward noun, like "Schedule" or "Cassette."

Obviously, something got lost in the translation. That happens a lot, I think. At Lent, for instance, we're asked to "deny ourselves," which everyone takes to mean self-sacrifice. But maybe not. Maybe "deny" here means "denial," as in Kubler-Ross' first stage of grief. You know, the kind of thing we self-actualized people are *not* supposed to do when seeking the truth.

Well, I say forget the truth. Trust your infinite capacity for self-deception. Hey, it's gotten you this far, hasn't it?

The Hardest Word

tem in the *Philadelphia Inquirer:* a minister in Easton, Pennsylvania, out for a Saturday walk as he prepared his Sunday sermon, was gunned down in cold blood by a deranged young man who had just broken up with his girlfriend. The shooting was without motive. The pastor left a wife and seven children.

"It was random, perverse," said the *Inquirer,* "one of those deeds that torments the logic of human existence."

Well, it's not the first time our logic has been tormented. Despite countless stories of triumphs and successes and ordinary heroes that cross our path each day, it's moments like these we remember: the twisted, the terrible, the Ted Bundys. More schoolchildren know Jeffrey Dahmer's name than Albert Schweitzer's.

But that's not what this story is about. After the shooting, the mother of the gunman put a notice in the paper, thanking friends and relatives for their support and asking for prayers for the minister's family. The minister's wife saw the notice, called the mother, and the two families met together and consoled one another.

"They're hurting just like us," the minister's wife said. Think of that.

Or think of this: after seven and a half *years* as a hostage, sometimes in isolation and nearly always in darkness, UPI Beirut correspondent Terry Anderson was released. In the intervening time, his father and brother had died. His baby daughter was born; already he had missed much of her childhood. With his journalist's gift for precision, he kept a careful mental calendar, always hyperaware of the endless days and unchanging nights.

Occasionally, he was threatened, sometimes beaten; he was told of his "imminent" release too, too many times. Most of human nature would have given up; some of his fellow hostages did exactly that, *willing* themselves to death. And, as the longest-held Western hostage, Anderson got to see it all—to witness those dying beside him, to watch those being released before him. He was his captors' most valuable pawn, though he could do nothing to make their world more just—well, nothing except suffer unspeakably.

And what did Terry Anderson say upon his release? *"As a Christian and a Catholic, it's required that I forgive."*

Oh, no, Terry, you're wrong, you're wrong. *Nothing* is required of you, except dying and paying taxes—and Uncle Sam might cut you a break on the latter. No, you had plenty of options: the option to lash out, to complain bitterly about the irrevocable time taken from you and your fatherless daughter; the option to call for revenge, a call that many would have supported; the option to blame the U.S. government, like many had before you; the option, certainly, to rail against God, who seemed to forsake you so completely; and—most merciful of all— you had the option to quit, to sink into the resignation and comfort of death, robbing your captors of their irreplaceable pawn.

No, you had choices—the same choices the minister's wife had. After 2,455 days of weighing the options, you *chose* forgiveness.

That's the problem with forgiveness: it requires choice. But that's not what we're told. We're told to "seek the truth," not forgiveness. It's a biblical message coopted by the New Agers. I heard one Crystal Pundit suggest that the only way to come to terms with one's past is to relentlessly seek the truth, even if that means "graveside confrontations," actually visiting your dead mother's tombstone and screaming epithets at her epitaph.

It's a national epidemic of truth-seeking. Whole books written on finding the "real you," or at least the inner child that used to be you. Geraldo wants "the truth" about Elvis (hint: he's dead), Oprah wants the facts on fat, Phil Donahue wants the truth about Devil-worshiping Nazi Felons Who Adopt Whales Through the Save the Whales Project—and then abuse them.

Well, in the face of this overwhelming movement—and in the face of the Bible itself—I offer an alternative view:

The truth won't do a damn thing.

It's a great myth, perpetrated by people who should know better. What would Terry Anderson gain, for instance, if he chose to dwell on the dark years of his captivity? The emptiness, the loneliness, the sheer senselessness of it all—and it's all *true,* isn't it? Or the minister's wife—could she ever stop grieving when she considers the truth of her new life alone: seven children to raise, with the comfort of her husband, her lover, and her best friend gone forever? And can one imagine the truth faced by the gunman's mother, whose own flesh and blood literally triggered this incalculable tragedy?

There's a movement afoot to rewrite parts of the Anglican *Book of Common Prayer.* There's only one section I'd change, Eucharistic Prayer C. I suggest they make it more realistic, to reflect the actual attitude of the congregation. Instead of

> ...*You blessed us with memory, reason and skill.*
> *But we turned against You,*
> *and turned against one another...*

Substitute the truth—well, the truth as we practice it:

> *Because You cursed us with memory,*
> *we forgot all about reason and skill.*
> *We remember and nurture every wound,*
>   *every slight,*
> *Until we turn against each other,*
> *and turn against You, the author of this mess...*

The truth is we hate the truth. If we're so eager to have the truth, then we should scream that fact from the mountaintops: "I have seen the truth, and I hate it!" Those rabid truth seekers would choke on their own medicine; imagine an entire culture of truth-seeking zealots, all of them proving just how unhealthy the truth can be.

In its stead, I offer this path to growth: learn to forget. Pray for a poor memory. Ask God for blinders.

I know what you're thinking: if Freud were alive today, he'd be rolling over in his grave. If psychology has proven anything, it's the crippling effect of repression. The shrinks' couches are overflowing with broken spirits who have blocked out the horrifying truth of their earlier lives. Unable to reclaim their past, they cannot face the future. If you don't believe the mind is capable of such deceit, watch the veterans at the Vietnam Memorial in Washington, D.C. Watch as the price of repression unfolds before you.

But I said *forgetting*, not repression. Repression is an unconscious act, a merciful method of self-preservation. Forgetting is conscious: "Hey, that sawbuck you owe me—forget it." Forgetting acknowledges the truth, then lets it go. Forgetting is choice, active and deliberate. Try as he might, Terry Anderson could no more repress those seven years than he could change the phases of the moon. Instead, he *chooses* to forget, then to forgive, allowing him to be free. Truly free.

Of course, there's another word for all of this: faith. Faith ignores the limits of truth. By believing in the unknowable, we're saved from the chains of the observable. It's an argument as old as Kierkegaard: We need a Savior to inform humanity of its predicament. It's not a truth we hold innately, rather it's a truth we abhor because of the demands it makes. It requires a leap of faith, because such faith runs counter to every human impulse: the impulse to seek out and punish the guilty, even if the guilty is us; the impulse to run like hell from who we are, or from the world; the impulse to believe in sweet, small packages like "the truth will make me free," when we know that the truth is only half the story, a half-truth.

It's forgiveness that will set us free—well, freer. Free enough to function each day, free enough to relearn an old word like *mercy*. When Jesus, on his cross and breathing his last, said, "Father, forgive them, for they know not what they do," it was the ultimate example of forgetting. *Of course* they knew what they did—they *nailed* him to a cross, for Christ's sake. This was no accident. But he overlooked that, his absolution more universal than the moment.

So if you want the truth, I offer no words of encouragement, save these: good luck.

But if you want a new life, I offer a new cliché: Forget, so you may forgive.

—*Thanks to Michael Wolf*

SPORTS AND GAMES have ruined my life. I have tennis elbow, runner's knee, and skier's hip—and that's just from *watching* sports.

Needless to say, few endeavors are more subject to change than sports. The booking industry in Las Vagas, for instance, has built its multibillion dollar industry on people's ridiculous attraction to the changing fortunes of professional teams. Michael Jordan pulls up lame, and suddenly the spread is shaved by three points and foreign affairs will disappear off the front page of *USA Today* for at least a week.

Like any active addict, I feel the need to explain my compulsive behavior. And this is the best explanation I've come up with yet, because it has the added benefit of being true.

Sports

Most couples fight over sex or money; if my wife and I divorce, it will be over sports. What started as an above-average relationship has deteriorated into hurtful silence. Sandee runs three to four miles, four times a week (She stopped two weeks to have a baby, then started again.) and watches sports year round. I play dek hockey and softball and watch an equal amount of baseball, football, and basketball. Few hospitalized neurotics are more obsessive.

So why do we fight? Every morning one of us will say, "Why did you let me watch all fourteen innings of the Indians-Brewers game till two in the morning? What do I care about a league with designated hitters?" Or "Why did you let me jog (or play hockey) yesterday? I told you my knees ache." To which the spouse replies, "Hey, you're a big boy/girl now—I'm not your mother/father." So, we seethe as our hurts become emotional as well as physical. Guilt, Ben-Gay, and coffee: the breakfast of champions.

Why do we subject ourselves to such punishment? Why do we watch all three and a half hours of *Monday Night Football,* all the while complaining loudly about how rotten both teams are? Why do we play seventeen innings of softball at the company picnic when our cartilage has all the elasticity of copper tubing? Mother Nature sends all of her oracles of warning—the muscle strain while moving boxes in the attic, the wry neck, the trick knees—but do we listen? My physical therapist drives a Mercedes with a license plate that reads THNX•MARK.

And clearly our national priorities are out of proportion. More people attend sporting events than participate in the national election. The networks spend more money covering the Olympics than covering Congress. People who cannot remember their state representative could easily name four out of the last five heavyweight boxing champions, or the entire 1968 Cardinals lineup (let's see, Javier, Maxvill, Cepeda...).

So what's the attraction? It would be easy to dismiss this madness as some kind of cultural genetic deficiency, but look at soccer. Around the world, fans will spend their life savings for a seat at the World Cup, where they earn the right to get the tar beat out of them. If it's genetic, then it's poisoned the whole species.

Here's my guess: it's all part of our search for God.

Euclid and Newton gave us the geometry and laws of bodies in motion: stresses, forces, torque, and gravity. As our fourteen-month-old daughter begins to walk, she learns hard lessons of hard science: when an irresistible force (my daughter's noggin) meets an immovable object (the refrigerator door), it hurts.

Nature teases us as adolescents with agility and prowess, but we peak quickly, unappreciative of our gifts and talents until they're mostly gone. So now it's every week at the YMCA, playing three-on-three basketball with others past their prime, our joints wrapped in swaddling clothes, trying to outsmart the natural course of things, trying to rediscover—what? Why are we risking life and limb? What are we looking for when we watch mindless hours of grown men playing children's games for obscene salaries?

We're looking for grace. We're looking for that one moment in eighth grade when we faked our way around Joey Marsip (who, at age thirteen, was six-feet-four) and our reverse lay-up found the hoop. We're remembering the gym class when Doris Chutka (who, at eighty-eight pounds dripping wet, could outrun anybody) turned around one fine day to find us at her right shoulder, our miraculous legs pumping toward the discarded football sleds which served as the finish line. We had found the second wind that cocky Doris had forgotten. For one unbelievable moment, our bodies were transcendent, muscles and joints and bones and blood working in a rhythm as sweet as a metronome. Doris would win every rematch, but it didn't matter; she was merely accomplishing the predictable while we became the legend, the unnamed fastest-in-the-school because we once beat Doris Chutka.

We don't watch sports for the expected, but the unexpected. Vic Wertz hits the ball four hundred feet to straightaway center—at least a double, probably a triple, maybe even—wait a minute, where did Mays come from? What's Havlichek doing with the basketball? Is Navratilova hiding a cannon in her racquet? But Lemieux *couldn't* have scored—he's lying on his back. We're cheering the sudden triumph over natural vectors. Michael Jordon's escape from gravity is *our* escape, even if it's temporary and vicarious. Tomorrow we'll drag ourselves to work, groggy from too little sleep but eager to share that shared moment of divinity with other addicts around the water cooler. "Did you *see* that play?"

God made us in his own image, Genesis tells us, but we know the truth. God made us poor imitators, fettered by physics and aging. Our experience with the spiritual rarely results in complete conversion but in small victories, the tiny moments that lift us heavenward, above our limits, above our dreams, above our vision, where we can finally touch the face of....

The backboard. Just once. That's all I ask. Really.

—*For Dean M.*

WHAT MEAN JOKES YOU PLAY, LIFE! Dust, ashes, rot. Surfacing from the magical bottom of childhood, from the warm, radiant depths, we open our chilled fist in the cold wind—and what have we brought up with us besides sand?

TATYANA TOLSTAYA
ON THE GOLDEN PORCH

Maybe We Ain't That Young Anymore

It's only eight o'clock on this warm summer evening in Fairmont, West Virginia, but the Playoff Nite Club is hopping. Unable to unwind from a day of dodging the moonscape called I-79, I stop in for a nightcap.

"Are you twenty-one?" the bouncer asks. I consider showering him with kisses of gratitude (I haven't seen twenty-one since the Carter administration) but show him my driver's license instead. The bouncer stamps the topside of my hand (*How odd,* I think), then squeezes three dollars out of me for a cover charge.

The outside of the bar is deceptive: a simple brick building, a couple of beer signs, and a bright blue-and-white awning. But inside it's bedlam—a long narrow room packed wall-to-wall with large-screen TVs, crowded booths, and people, people, people. (Is the Grateful Dead in town?) With that many folks, you'd expect to see all sorts of sizes and shapes. Well, it's true of the women, but the men are all tall. (Okay, taller than me.) After a few minutes of standing nose-to-shoulder blades with several crew-cut gentlemen, I realize they're a *lot* taller than me.

Miraculously, despite all the people, there's hardly a line at the bar. (*How odd*, I think again.) After paying three dollars (!) for a beer (!!), I finally find a standing spot near the dance floor.

It's hard not to think of myself as an outsider, feeling self-conscious as I stand alone in a strange bar. Of course, it's hard to think *at all*. The music is so loud (made louder by reverberations off the brick walls), you'd think the Irish Republican Army was holding a reunion outside.

But I *am* thinking. I'm thinking how little things have changed. I hung out in bars like this nearly two decades ago. The music was disco, the clothes were polyester, and the shoes had platforms, but it was still the same scene. All the players are still here: the two overweight women dancing together, shuffling so they don't move too much; the tall girl with the bare midriff and the short girl with the tight jeans dancing together; the couples dancing together, the self-conscious white guys and their uninhibited dates; and a few oddballs who *should* feel inhibited but don't. All that's needed is gold jewelry and flared pants and soon you'd have a Capricorn comparing mood rings with a Gemini.

Despite ten thousand similarities (there's even the requisite drunk guy who's managed to guzzle too much beer at three bucks a pop), something is different here, something doesn't fit.

Suddenly it sinks in. It's me. *I* don't fit in.

I am the oldest (and possibly shortest) guy here. As a stranger to this bar, I expected an occasional sidelong glance, but now I realize I'm suspect because I'm old, not because I'm a foreigner. The gray hair. The sensible shoes. The pants from Sears. *Old*. Born in a time before cable, before Monday Night Football, before *banking machines*, for God's sake. What I'm feeling is suspicion. The yippies might have said it first, but it's an attitude as old as adolescence itself: Never trust anyone over thirty.

Finally, I summon the type of courage I haven't needed since I was single.

"Excuse me," I say (well, scream) to the pretty girl standing near me, "but is everyone here over twenty-one?"

She looks at me as if I had just spoken Swahili. "No," she shouts back. "Just eighteen. You only have to be twenty-one if you want to drink." She drops her eyes to my hand and smiles. "Like you."

She was glancing at my black stamp. It identifies me as over-twenty-one, as over-the-hill, as no one to talk to. The girl turns her head, finds a friend among the crowd, waves quickly to me and scampers away—you know, away from *Dad*. The stamp might as well be an *A* for *Adult*. Or *B* for *Boring*.

Thirtysomething and washed-up, right?

Funny, but I don't feel old. Well, older than these folks, with their high-top tennis shoes and fifty-dollar haircuts. And I'm too old to dance to this music, which sounds remarkably like my Gibson washer did just before the gasket blew. But I'm not too old to be here, to enjoy myself. I'm not too old to live vicariously, to savor the endless energy of those on the dance floor. I'm not so old that I live in the past, judging others by the arbitrary standard of my own generation. I can still see the similarities, the common ground. If I look closely enough, those are my parents out there, taking a spin to Glenn Miller's "String of Pearls." And if I look *real* close, I can see my infant daughter, Faith, grooving to some twenty-first century technopop.

"All my life's a circle," the decidedly nondisco Harry Chapin sang twenty years ago:

"All my life's a circle, but I can't tell you why—
The seasons spinning 'round again,
The years keep rolling by..."

I finish my three-dollar beer, smile at the pretty girl who scampered away, and leave the Playoff Lounge. Back at the hotel, I jot down a short note on Country Club Motor Lodge stationery. It's a reminder to myself, as well as to my infant daughter.

Remember to tell Faith: always be nice to the old guy standing alone near the dance floor. He could be someone's dad. A kind word from you is all he needs to make his beer taste less bitter.

"JESUS IS NOT SAFELY CONFINED in the first century. He is our contemporary, proclaiming release to the captives and rebelling against all who silently accept the structures of injustice. If he is not in the ghetto, if he is not where men are living at the brink of existence, but is, rather, in the easy life of the suburbs, then the gospel is a lie" (James Cone).

It's fitting that my journey would begin with the birth of our first daughter and end (well, stop for a while) with the birth of our second. Both were born into safe, open arms, which puts them among the globe's minority. Our living rooms are stacked so high with toys and clothes we can't see out the window into our own backyard, where a thousand million children await our leftovers. Upon their shoulders our comfy world is built; for good or bad, that's the legacy we pass to the next generation.

Hope and Denzell

The *Metro Orange Line* subway in Washington, D.C., is a demographer's dream. I board the *Metro* in Vienna, Virginia, the first leg on my journey to D.C. General Hospital. In the next forty-five minutes, we pass through a cross-section of every American city, from the white suburbs through the changing border towns to the heart of urban life. By the Stadium-Armory stop, just south of the U.S. Capitol, I'm one of two Caucasians left on the train car.

Ten minutes later I'm walking through the labyrinthine corridors of D.C. General. Many of the rooms here are testament to the price of metropolitan living. The hospital sees nearly two thousand "blunt traumas" in its emergency room each year, many of them shootings and stabbings from D.C.'s drug kingdom. More than a third of the hospital's resources are spent on the consequences of substance abuse: fights, accidents, overdoses, care for HIV-positive patients. Armed guards stand watch at several rooms, where prisoners from Lorton Prison and the D.C. Jail receive treatment. I'm only twenty miles from Vienna, Virginia, but it seems much farther than that.

Finally, I reach my destination: 2 East, the boarder baby nursery. "Boarder baby" is a new, disturbing phrase in the lexicon. These are urban children born to mothers who are too sick, too addicted, or too AWOL to either care for their babies or to sign them over to foster homes. Instead, these infants live in a legal limbo: medically cleared to go home, but with no home to go to.

To date (mostly since the advent of crack cocaine), scores of boarder babies have been born at D.C. General and nearby Howard University Hospital. D.C.'s foster-care system—the logical safety net for such cases—is too overloaded to handle these special infants. If adoptive parents express an interest in a certain infant, the swamped courts can find a way to expedite the matter. But many of these babies are drug-exposed, making them less appealing to prospective parents (not to mention the possibility of the real mother returning at any moment). Later—by the time the babies start to walk—they'll be transferred to transitional homes to await a spot in a permanent foster home, or else be reunited with the mother or another relative. Until then, these limbo babies will spend their first ten months or so in a hospital ward, with a cadre of competent, well-meaning medical personnel to feed and clothe them, but always as surrogates.

In the foyer outside 2 East, I gown up and wash my hands to reduce the risk of infection for both the babies and myself. Inside the ward, the eight cribs are arranged in a horseshoe, with three baby swings in the middle of the room. The lights are low, the drapes are half drawn, and no mobiles are in sight—all part of an effort to keep stimulation to a minimum. It's a shared trait among drug- and alcohol-exposed babies to easily overload on stimulation.

The first child I meet is Babette's Baby Girl. (Two of the eight children have never received their own name.) She sits quietly in her baby swing, her black eyes wide and unblinking. She has a face only a mother could love—thin and bony, with her nose and ears in odd angle to the rest of her features. But those enormous eyes make up for everything else. Her pupils are black holes, both literally and figuratively: they suck in every reflection, every vision, every new face. She latches on to my face, and won't change her stare until I offer her my pinky. She reaches with both hands, struggling to put my finger in her mouth; but somewhere in the synapses of her brain the message is garbled, so she abandons my hand in favor of her own.

Next to Babette's Baby Girl is Chloe. She's been sitting up in her swing for an hour without fussing—a new record, says Beverly Rountree, a 2 East nurse. When I ask Ms. Rountree if these boarder babies remind her of her own grandchildren, she shakes her head. "These kids are different," she says.

Out in the hallway, on a thick hospital blanket, occupational therapist Chrystyne Babiak is working with ten-month-old Denzell. By ten months, most babies are experts at "push-ups"—lifting their chests off the floor and holding their heads high. But Denzell still struggles, either pushing with his hands too far outside or too inside to hold his torso steady. Though Denzell's technique is shaky, Ms. Babiak is pleased. Denzell was once thought to have fetal alcohol syndrome, which significantly delays development. Just a few months ago, he was behind in nearly every milestone category; now it looks like he'll learn to walk just about on schedule.

Despite Chrystyne Babiak's optimism and her professional commitment, all does not seem well at the nursery. Something seems off kilter here, not quite right. When I volunteer to return Denzell to his crib, I find the answer.

Boarder babies don't smile.

Well, rarely. After a solid minute of coaxing, I finally eke a smile out of Denzell. It's the first smile I've seen in an hour—one smile among six awake babies in sixty minutes. I'm no expert, but that is *not* normal behavior. In spite of the excellent care, there's a missing element here, like background music you notice for the first time. It's the sound of a bloodless heartbeat, a rain without rhythm, a tick without a tock. They get a warm bed, clean clothes, three squares a day (Denzell *loves* applesauce), plus exercise on the adjoining porch—*but so do the prisoners from the D.C. Jail.* As I discard my gown and hike back to my return trip on the *Orange Line,* I think: *Maybe boarder babies are smarter then they seem. Maybe they don't smile much because they know there just isn't much to smile about.*

Ten days later I'm dressed in a hospital gown again, this time holding my brand-new daughter, Hope. In a few days, my wife and I will take our daughter home. It's a scene borrowed from the millennia: proud parents and their shiny new child. But for every child like Hope, there's a child like Denzell, born without an even break, lurching and stumbling through childhood on the generosity of other folks, folks who can satisfy their physical needs but cannot be, can never be, their parents. It would take adoption to do that, and Denzell and his cribmates aren't high on anyone's adoption list. Despite each baby's unique story, all of 2 East's boarder infants share the same three strikes: all were conceived out of wedlock; all are dirt poor; and not a one of them has European blood.

Just like Jesus.

Think about it. Jesus today would've been a lousy bet for adoption. Dark Semitic looks, born to an incredibly young mother who claims she was impregnated by a spirit (coke-induced psychosis, no doubt), who gave birth to him in a place like D.C. General's emergency room because she didn't have healthcare coverage. Just another urban statistic. Shake your head; turn the page.

Or Moses—same story. His mother thought that by abandoning her son to the oppressors, he might have a better chance at life. Before we condemn the mothers of the babies in 2 East, think of *their* options.

If we can forget (albeit with difficulty) the unborn for just a moment, we must confront the reality of the forgotten postborn. Our world is cleaved between those born into the luxury and security of prenatal visits, a caring adult or two, and the buffer of money, versus the other seventy-five percent of the world born into stunning poverty. Unlike my wife and I, there are millions of parents who have no picture of Hope tucked inside their wallets.

There's simply no excuse for such a state, but we've made hundreds of them. And it's a damn good thing, too, because we'll need every one when we meet whomever awaits us at our very last subway stop at the end of the line. While we're arguing with the Conductor about the fare, Denzell will be playing with the other children on the crowded platform, finally happy, finally laughing, finally free.